# Food
## for Thought

# Food
## for Thought

**How the Creator of**
**Fuddrucker's,**
**Romano's Macaroni Grill,**
**and**
**eatZi's**
**Built a $10 Billion Empire**
**One Concept at a Time**

# PHILIP J. ROMANO

**Dearborn**™
Trade Publishing
A **Kaplan Professional** Company

President, Dearborn Publishing: Roy Lipner
Vice President and Publisher: Cynthia A. Zigmund
Acquisitions Editor: Jonathan Malysiak
Senior Project Editor: Trey Thoelcke
Interior Design: Lucy Jenkins
Cover Design: Design Solutions
Typesetting: the dotted i

Published by Dearborn Trade Publishing
A Kaplan Professional Company

Printed in the United States of America

05  06  07     10  9  8  7  6  5  4  3  2  1

**Library of Congress Cataloging-in-Publication Data**

Romano, Philip J.
    Food for thought : how the creator of Fuddrucker's, Romano's
    macaroni grill, and Eatzi's built a $10 billion empire one concept at
    a time / Philip J. Romano with Steve McLinden.
        p.      cm.
    Includes index.
    ISBN 1-4195-0008-2
    1. Romano, Phil.    2. Restaurateurs—Biography.    I. McLinden,
    Steve.   II. Title.
    TX910.5.R663R66  2005
    647.95′092—dc22
                                                        2004029800

# Contents

# The Phil Romano
# Operational Integrity Creed

**A** restaurant should be responsible. It must serve a purpose and fulfill a need. It must make the public happy. Customers must get their money's worth and be given value. A restaurant has to be self-motivating by nature and motivate both customers and employees.

A restaurant must be honest. It should clearly state what it does and then follow through to fulfill that promise. It can't say one thing, then be another. It must possess emotional intelligence and understand itself, too. It must have imagination and put a smile on people's faces, while letting them experience something they haven't experienced before.

Employees must demonstrate dignity to others and also be treated with dignity by restaurant ownership and management, in the same manner that ownership and management would like to be treated. The customer should be afforded the same dignity.

A restaurant and its management should demonstrate leadership abilities and provide a benchmark for other eating establishments.

A restaurant should take advantage of its success to give something back to the community. Its owners, operators, and employees should do their best to help make that community healthy and maintain a strong tax base, so that both the restaurant and the community will thrive.

# Prologue

It was late 1987 in San Antonio, and I was feeling restless and distracted. Christmas was fast approaching, but south Texas was still warm and muggy and I just couldn't get in the holiday spirit. At this point in my life, I should have been turning cartwheels. I was living a restaurateur's dream after all, or so people would tell me.

My 12th restaurant concept, Fuddrucker's, known as the home of the "The World's Greatest Hamburgers," had exploded and expanded all over the country. I'd brought it public, made a handsome sum, and built myself a spacious new house in the Dominion neighborhood, sweating side by side with the workers every day, hammering and laying bricks, and probably pissing off the construction foreperson to no end. I named it "The House That Hamburgers Built," only in Latin.

People were telling me, "Relax, Phil. Kick back. Start enjoying life." Tennis, golf, painting, vacationing, partying, decorating that new house: These pastimes would keep me more than busy, they insisted. Still, I was getting fidgety for something new to do, something to create, and the itch just wouldn't go away. I began to acknowledge what my subconscious had been trying to tell me for months: The life of empty leisure is not for me. In short, I was going crazy doing nothing.

About this time, the restaurant world began buzzing about this restaurant chain, Olive Garden, that was enjoying a great deal of success and good press. One afternoon, after an uninspired morning of Christmas shopping, I pulled into one for lunch.

Certainly, the Olive Garden served up a serviceable meal: lots of salad, soup, and bread and reliable entrees in fair portions. But the food wasn't that good and definitely not authentic. As I glanced around at the faux Italian décor, I had to flinch. The waiter must have thought I had indigestion. He asked: "Is everything all right, sir?" I nodded halfheartedly.

The thing is, I didn't feel like I was in an Italian restaurant. Yet people were gravitating there in big numbers. There was a din, a clatter. But I looked around for the kitchen and got a little nervous. I couldn't find it. You couldn't see how the food was being prepared. What's to hide?

Olive Garden, I realized, was an Italian restaurant created by a corporation. Now, I'm an authentic Italian, and I already know how to create restaurants. If Olive Garden could do these all over the country, there was no telling what I could do, I thought. It takes Italians to make things truly Italian and *Romano* is about as Italian as you can get.

As I finished my meal, I started daydreaming—one of my favorite pastimes. My mind drifted back to the kitchen table of my youth in upstate New York. Most of the homes in our neighborhood didn't have dining rooms, including ours. But the Romano kitchen table was extra large, and we always seemed to have an abundance of family and friends gathered around, making lively conversation and sampling my mother's savory sauces and the other goodies that she was preparing just a few feet away from our curious noses.

She'd drape the table with a white tablecloth and fresh-cut flowers. Then my grandfather would plop down a gallon jug of his homemade wine, a fine vintage direct from the cellar. As we chatted, we would dip fresh-out-of-the-oven Italian bread in olive oil and nibble on it. These were warm, animated gatherings, often punctuated by emotional outpourings and happy shouts, accompanied by Italian sonatas playing on the old family phonograph in the living room. It was comforting, warm, and familiar.

If I could somehow project this childhood experience into a restaurant, by putting people in the middle of a giant "kitchen" with a jug of wine and letting them experience those wonderful, authentic tastes and smells and that family-friendly atmosphere, then just think how people would react. As a full-blooded Italian, I could offer them a level of authenticity that should make them go "Wow!", and something every good new concept needs: a distinct point of difference.

That was, in retrospect, a landmark moment in the creation of a concept I would later bring to life: Romano's Macaroni Grill. I immediately started putting the place together in my mind. As luck would have it, I'd pinpointed the perfect spot for this future creation a few weeks earlier, just outside of San Antonio in Leon Springs.

More importantly, I was feeling alive again. There was a bounce in my step as I shot out the door of corporate "Italy" that afternoon. On my way home, I began devising my strategy for my then-unnamed concept and felt an honest-to-goodness smile spreading across my face for the first time in a long time.

I realized that my real hobby, my vocation, and my one true love were all one in the same: creating restaurants and breathing life into things that make people's lives a little richer. And I haven't stopped doing what I love. I still see the world through the eyes of an excited child. And now, late in life, I have a new "concept" that I know will be the best of all: my own son, Sam.

The values that distinguish my restaurant creations are the ones I hope to instill in him as a good, productive human being: truth, integrity, honor, passion, responsibility, imagination, and generosity. The world has been good to me, and I'd like to help convey my gratitude through Sam and make this a textbook for him as well as for everyone who has eaten in or owned a restaurant. I am 65 years old at this writing, after all, so there's a chance I may not be here when Sam, who is now 9, gets through college, goes into business, and has a family of his own. Sam, I think I may have found a way to nag you from the grave!

# 1

# EARLY DAYS

### F o o d   f o r   T h o u g h t

People don't want the same old thing, the same way, the same taste.
They want the excitement of experiencing something different,
something new, something they have never seen before.

I am what some call an Italian's Italian. The son of Italian immigrant parents, I was born Philip James Romano on Columbus Day in 1939 to Rose and Samuel Romano, and I was raised in an Italian Catholic neighborhood in upstate New York. But the story of how I got to where I am is more of a classic American tale. It starts with my grandfather, Philip, who was the first of my ancestors to blaze a trail from Italy to the United States.

Philip, who was born in Castna, Geavoni—now called Enora, Sicily—arrived alone at Ellis Island in 1907 with little more than the clothes on his back. But he had broken out in a mysterious rash during his journey, and the immigration authorities turned him back. "We can't take you. Rash. Sorry." And that was that.

But Grandpa Philip wasn't about to let a skin eruption ruin his American dream. Undaunted, he traveled to Argentina, where he worked as a carpenter and saved nearly all his wages. Two years later, rash free, he returned to Italy and retrieved my grand-mother Rosalie, and their son, Samuel, along with two of his brothers and a sister. They boarded another ship to New York, had a healthy journey, and cleared immigration.

Grandpa promptly went to work as a carpenter, building his business from the ground up and serving as an inspiration to the Romanos for generations.

I was the first one in our family to be born in America. Until I was about six years old, I hardly saw my father. He was in the Navy in World War II for nearly three years, stationed in Pearl Harbor after the attack. Grandpa Philip raised me while he was gone. My grandfather was an earnest, humble man who never drove a car and spoke only Italian. But he did pretty well for himself and for the rest of us, and I could understand him most of the time, especially when he said in his native tongue, "I live to eat."

I wasn't much for reading or writing or articulation early in my life, and my efforts to try to figure out what Grandpa was try-ing to communicate helped me learn valuable lessons about how to get my point across nonverbally.

Mama Rose was a loving, understanding woman with a great sense of humor. She was also a terrific cook, like most of my family members. She would absolutely light up the room when she came in. She'd say: "Talk of the devil and he will appear, talk about failure and it will happen, talk about success and you'll have it." So my sister, Rosalie, and I knew what not to conjure up unless we wanted to catch hell. Only later would I come to grasp the "success" part of that equation.

But my father was my hero. He was a wise man and great role model, even in absentia those early years. He'd write and send me pictures, and I would show them to everyone and brag that my father was a war hero. When he returned, I clung to him. He took me fishing and hunting and we talked constantly, I went just about everywhere with him, even to work. After all those years apart, I was afraid to let him out of my sight.

My parents met while working in the Dunn and McCarthey shoe factory in Auburn, New York. Dad was a machinist and handyman there and was especially quick to fix my mother's machine when it broke down. He finally asked a coworker to introduce them formally, and they really hit it off, marrying on July 4, 1934. Fireworks ensued.

My mom was a little thing. She weighed 89 pounds. I weighed 12 pounds when I was born! That's why I tell people that I'm not Italian, I'm Caesarian. "The problem I have when I leave the house," I'd say, "is I don't know whether to go out the door . . . or the window." That may explain my unconventional approach to life today. Because I was born on Columbus Day, I used to ask my mother why she didn't name me Christopher. "I couldn't," she'd reply. "The milkman's name was Christopher."

My parents lived in a small apartment and often worked 12-hour days. After I came along, my father created a second job for himself, repairing small appliances for people in the neighborhood. He was very creative and could do anything with his hands, even build a house from the ground up. He proudly stood behind his work and was quick to make things right if he erred. He settled in as an electrician.

So that's how I came to grow up in a small house in little ethnic enclave in Auburn, New York, and never knew anyone other than Italian Catholics existed until I was about 12. Boy, did I have a surprise coming! We had just one car in the family, and my dad took it to work. In those days, if family members wanted to go out for dinner or entertainment, they all had to go together, and I think that kept our family and other families of that era together. Though we struggled, I never really felt poor when I was growing up, because my parents had strong, enduring value systems.

Knowing I'd have to find my own way through life, my father would point things out to me in our time together but let me draw my own conclusions. He never came out and said "Philip, now don't do this and don't do that." That was for me to figure out. For example, he'd point to a man leaning against a wall and say, "He can't stand on his own two feet to work." Or we'd go out to lunch and he'd see some guys he knew on coffee break, then single one out to me and say, "Watch him. He's never going to put his hand in his pocket to help pay the bill." I watched. He was right. "There are just some guys with fish-hooks in their pockets," he said. It was like having a lesson in thinking.

While the elders of the family spoke fluent Italian, I never learned to speak it. It was the same way with all my Italian friends. Our parents said that when we went to school, we were going to be American Italians, not Italian Americans. In this country, this was what we needed to be, they emphasized. They didn't want me to go to school and speak with an accent.

I was constantly in trouble in school—a chronic daydreamer. When the teachers were talking, I'd sit quietly in class staring straight at them, but in truth I'd be miles away, thinking about something, somewhere, or someone else. They eventually caught on to my thousand-yard stare and gave me hell for it. These same teachers were fond of telling me that I'd never amount to anything. In fact, my mother would get more than her share of angry calls from the principal's office. I felt like mom and I went to grade school together, because she'd always come to the school and stand up for me.

"Philip's grades are low, his spelling is atrocious, and his attention span is short. I just can't teach him. I am so worried about this boy's future," one teacher told her. My mother replied: "Well, ma'am, I am not worried about Philip's future. And what do you mean, 'Can't teach him'? You're the teacher. Teach him!"

God bless her, she never yelled at me for poor academics, and like many protective moms, she may have given me a bit of a false impression of myself, because her boy could do no wrong in her eyes. She spoiled me and I let her do it, of course. I loved both my parents equally, but to this day, if I have a stomachache at night, it's my mother I'm calling. She taught me some key lessons through all of this: the value of unconditional love and loyalty and the merits of patience with your children.

In the fifth grade, I walked over to the house of a friend, Johnny Rio, after school one day and we were both toting our report cards. His mother, a nice lady but a strict disciplinarian, looked at his and saw a bunch of As and Bs. Then she looked at mine and scowled. In fact, it was so bad that she told Johnny he couldn't play with me anymore. (We managed to circumvent her, and we're good friends to this day.)

My father would get a little short with me about my studies, even though I had never actually failed a grade. My school, I should point out, was the same place he had gone to school. In fact, we had a lot of the same teachers. Because I never learned good study habits from my parents, who didn't finish school themselves, I seldom did homework. Their idea of "homework" for me was washing dishes and mowing the lawn. I later found out from my teachers that my father used to skip school and go down to the town dump and blast rats with a BB gun. Ha! Now I was armed with the perfect comeback the next time he reprimanded me about my schooling: "Daddy," I told him one day, smirking. "Miss Burdock said I act just like you."

I used to tell my teachers that I didn't need school and that my father didn't even graduate, "and look how well he's doing and how smart he turned out to be." But they said if my father had finished school, just think how much smarter he would be. They also told me how much further I would get in life if I finished. I'm grateful to this day for the advice.

In seventh grade, most of my friends and I transferred to a new Catholic school that was better suited to working around my shortcomings and accentuating my creative skills. We went on field trips to Niagara Falls and to historical places, and I really started thinking for the first time that, my God, there is a big world outside of Auburn, and someday I'm going to conquer it.

My dad always told me that, whatever I decided to do, I should be the best at it. "If you're gonna have a hot dog stand, have the biggest and best hot dog stand it the world. If you're gonna sell shoes, sell the best. If you're a bum, then be the world's most famous bum—one they're gonna write about. Be known near and far for what you are." He was in essence saying, "Philip, have a point of difference in your life. Be your own man and rise above the ordinary. Wow the crowd. Whatever you do, do it better than anyone else." Good advice! It still governs me today.

Family respect was always a key component of my upbringing. On holidays and other special occasions, we'd gather at someone's house, drink Grandpa's homemade wine, and eat a wonderful variety of Italian food and Americanize it with some hamburgers and hot dogs. I'd see how other parents would talk about their families and often overhear tales about the misdoings of someone's son or daughter and horror stories of how they dishonored their families. I told myself I was never going to put my mother or father through that. No one was going to hear my name spoken in shameful tones. So I resolved that I would do my best to uphold the family honor.

# 2

# BUSINESS BEGINNINGS— GETTING OUT OF THE BOX

### F o o d   f o r   T h o u g h t

Do something that is different and do it better than anyone else
in the business. I call it my "point of difference" and
it governs virtually everything I've done in my life. I'd rather
fail at something new, exciting, and different than succeed
at something ordinary. Understand your point of difference,
and make it the basis for your brand.

**M**y out-of-the-box, or should I say off-the-porch, approach to business began at an early age. Because my parents were of modest means, I never dreamed of asking them for an allowance. If I wanted something, I had to earn it myself.

When I was a kid in Auburn, you had to buy a newspaper route to get into the delivery business. So I picked up one for a whopping $9 from a kid named Marshall Bingham. It was a 96-customer afternoon route I could do after school, so I took it over and started out making about $10 a week. My only obligation was to throw the papers onto subscribers' front porches.

But when winter approached, I had a brainstorm. After the first snow, I asked my customers if they'd pay me extra if I would put their paper between their storm doors and main doors in bad weather. It just didn't seem right to leave it on the porch in the snow, even though that was all I had to do. "You shouldn't have to tromp out there in the cold and wet yard to get to it," I told them during my pitch. Some paid 15 cents extra for this extra service and others paid as much as 50 cents—nice little bonuses for a 12-year-old. I ended up making twice my base pay on the route as a result of this value-added idea. And the customers also took a shine to me. Some ladies compensated me with brownies, hot chocolate, and other goodies for my efforts, which are mighty good wages, too.

I basically decided to let each of the customers put a value on what I was doing. I had become a young entrepreneur, though I had no idea what the word meant at the time, much less how to spell it. But I did realize that if I gave people something extra or unusual, I could parlay that into extra cash and a lot of goodwill. The point of difference that my father always stressed was already paying off. I was a paperboy with a twist. Noting my creative prowess and sundry moneymaking schemes I concocted in my youth, my neighborhood contemporaries soon tagged me with the nickname "Fabulous Phil."

I also set, or "stuck," bowling pins at an alley in Auburn as a kid and used that extra money to buy new clothing and savings bonds. You could buy a $25 bond then for $15. Five years later, I'd be able to buy my first car—a blue 1948 Mercury Coupe—with $125 in savings bonds and a small cache of dough I'd squirreled away from other odd jobs.

Our family moved from New York to Florida halfway through high school, and I played football for each school. People knew me in New York and knew what I was capable of doing, but I had to reengineer myself in Florida and prove myself all over again. As tough as that was, it was good preparation for my adult career. You can always reinvent yourself in a new location and come back better and stronger every time you do.

I also played baseball and basketball but excelled most as a hard-hitting linebacker on the football field, even attracting the attention of college scouts. At the time, there was a draft, and it seemed like half of the guys in my class joined the Army Reserves right after graduation. As a requirement of the Reserves, you had to spend six months in active duty. So I missed about a semester and half doing my Reserves stint. Instead of going off to a university, I went to Palm Beach Junior College and continued to fulfill my military obligation there.

After a year at the Palm Beach college, UCLA flew me out to Los Angeles for a football tryout. They liked what they saw but wanted to red-shirt me—that is, hold off a year while I grew a little bigger, older, and stronger. So I turned them down. I did play a little semipro football there for the Van Nuys All-Stars, and they were a bruising bunch.

In retrospect, it was a good thing I went into the Army before starting college, because it built up my self-confidence and taught me how to take orders and how to give them. I came out a trained killer and I didn't let anything or anyone intimidate me. Now that's a point of difference!

I became president of the Esquire Club at Palm Beach Junior College, an organization that included every male student on campus, and I also was president of my fraternity, Chi Sigma. In those leadership roles, I had some clout. If I thought things had to be addressed or changed at school, then I'd play a union leader role and take the issues to school authorities. For example, we had restrictions on what we could wear to school: no Bermuda shorts and no T-shirts. I applied pressure to help get that dress code changed. I also went to the Jaycees of the nearby town of Lake Worth to create a scholarship for a member of my fraternity, selling them on the notion that we were the future of the community, standard bearers for the school, etc. They were sold.

But the president of the college, Dr. Maynard, stood in our way. He said we just couldn't create a scholarship that wasn't accessible to all of the students. We argued about it, and a big controversy ensued. I had to threaten to hire a lawyer before he finally said, "Ah, hell, do it." I wasn't the least bit shy about butting heads with the dean.

I had another run-in with the administrator. This was during the early rock-and-roll days, and I had seen an opportunity in promoting a good little greaser band at fraternity and sorority gigs around the college. We were paying them $50 per performance, and they were getting a nice following. At one sorority function, we had between 600 and 700 students show up at $2 a head, so we ended up clearing about $1,000 for our fraternity— not bad money for the time.

The sorority members who hosted the party found out about my windfall and demanded the money from me. I told them "no dice"—a popular phrase at the time—so they went to Maynard to complain. We couldn't settle it, so he referred us to the school's interfraternity council. They heard the case and let us keep the money. Free enterprise won out.

Ironically, Dr. Maynard came to me about 20 years later and asked me to serve on the board at the college. I declined the good dean's invitation, but I later decided to be a good sport and serve in an advisory capacity to the school. I suppressed the urge to say, "Yeah, but it'll cost you $1,000 bucks."

I had other little business ventures in college. As a sophomore, I started a carpet-cleaning business with a friend, Buddy Blount, using rented equipment that we carted around in an old Volkswagen van. But we made the mistake of deviating from our specialty and agreed to clean a set of very expensive drapes for a well-to-do woman just before an important cocktail party. Not really experts on sensitive fabric, we proceeded to totally ruin them—and ruin our short-lived business. True, we offered a memorable point of difference but not the kind that poor woman had in mind.

I transferred to Florida Atlantic University and opened two little martial arts schools. I had boxed in the Army, an extension of a survival skill I'd picked up as a kid. In fourth grade, a kid named Copes who lived near the neighborhood store started picking on me. Although he hadn't gotten too mean with me yet, I was determined to be ready if he did. So I filled up one of my father's Navy duffel bags with rags, hung it up in the cellar, and proceeded to whale on it relentlessly every day. I visualized what I would do to this kid if he pushed me too far. He never did. As I got bigger and quicker and stronger and smarter, I lost many of my fears. But after the Army, I had no desire to end up punch-drunk. So I moved on to karate, studying with some of the masters and competing in meets around the country. I earned a black belt in judo and a second-degree black belt in karate, then parlayed this knowledge into teaching. I was intent on maintaining a tough-guy image, too, so the schools were a natural extension.

Here I was, a young student, making $18,000 to $20,000 a year with the two schools I owned, which was more than some of my instructors and professors were earning. Little did I dream that, instead of serving up kicks and punches, I'd someday be serving up food and drink to thousands from coast to coast.

During the summer, while still a member of the Army Reserves, I did a stint with the Florida Power and Light Company, working my ass off digging power-pole holes. The job was a grind, and I began to worry that I would be doing this the rest of my life. But even the most boring jobs can hold creative opportunity. Florida Power rewarded employees who came up with solutions to recurring problems. They had a safety program in which they'd gather workers together and discuss procedures for helping injured employees in various scenarios. The question came up of how to best assist a line worker if he got jolted while up on a pole. Various workers responded that you'd immediately call an ambulance, get him down as soon as it was safe, give him mouth-to-mouth resuscitation, etc. I told them, "Why don't you go up there with an oxygen bottle that's small enough to carry in your hand, strap the oxygen to his face, and then bring him down. Why wait to get him on the ground to render aid?" They liked the idea and adopted it, and I got a nice cash award. But I thought, "My God, hasn't anybody thought of that incredibly simple solution before?" The approach, novel at the time, is commonplace.

I've come to learn that creativity is mostly about identifying a problem and, instead of just living with it, coming up with a solution. Too many companies are resigned to working around problems instead of really addressing their cause. Anybody can train themselves to be creative thinkers in that sense of the term. It just happens that some are naturally better at it.

My pole-truck foreman, Red, had an odd lunchtime habit that he practiced as we all sat around with our sack lunches. Red, a married guy with a couple of kids, would pull out his sandwich, take a bite, and say, "Ah, dammit, egg-salad again," then throw it on the ground. I saw him do this several times. One day, I finally said, "Red, why don't you get your wife to make you something else?" He said, "My wife? I made 'em!" True story. I thought, geez, sometimes it's tough to solve a problem if you're the cause of it.

Probably the craziest job I worked during my college days was as an assistant to a private investigator named Jack Harwood. Jack specialized in insurance fraud, like exposing a guy who's out playing golf when he claims to have a bad back, and messy divorces. At that time, spouses had to have significant evidence against their better (or worse) half to win a divorce. So we followed cheating spouses around, often to lovers' rendezvous at hotels and motels.

After the couple went in, we'd wait a little while, then knock down the door and take pictures. Jack always held the camera, and I was supposed to protect him as well as the camera. If the guy got up, I'd just knock him back down. One time, a guy bolted out of bed, then jumped out of a second-story window. Another time, a huge naked guy chased me out of a motel room and down a hallway. He cornered me and started throwing punches. I held my ground and swung back, but he ducked and I put my fist through a window. Ouch. We also followed a few mobsters around town, sometimes at high speed. Jack and I would puncture a taillight with an ice pick to make the car easier to follow at night. How's that for risky business? I'm lucky an ice pick wasn't used to puncture me. Harwood was a gutsy guy and an amusing fellow with whom I stayed in touch until his death a few years ago.

I never graduated from Florida Atlantic by the way, even though I had more than 168 total semester hours and all I lacked was 6 hours of foreign language. I paid for my own education, so I just took what I wanted and studied things that intrigued me. I started taking courses with the thought of becoming a teacher and head coach someday. But I never went back to get my degree, in part because newer, better business opportunities were starting to present themselves. Today, I give lectures at colleges.

# 3

# NOW I'M COOKING

F o o d   f o r   T h o u g h t

It's not the sweet smell of success that drives me; it's the fear of
failure. But I never let the fear of failure stop me from doing
something new and different.

In 1965, I sold my karate schools
and opened my first restaurant, The Gladiator, in Lake Park,
Florida, near West Palm Beach. I entered into a partnership
with a guy whose son had been taking karate lessons from me.
It was the all-American boy's dream: the fast-paced, fantastic
food and beverage business. All the food you could eat, all the
beer and cocktails you could consume, and all the girls you
could meet. I was 24 and on top of the world. And my eatery's
name, The Gladiator, kept my tough-guy thing going.

This might be a shocker, but I will confess here that I had
never worked in a restaurant before I owned one. In fact, I take
great pride in the fact that, since college, I've never relied on
anyone but myself for a paycheck, never had a real job, and, in
my mind, never actually worked a day in my life.

Fortunately, I had my family recipes to fall back on. At The
Gladiator, my own Italian restaurant, you could get a meatball

sandwich for 69 cents, a spaghetti dinner for $1.49, and a full steak dinner for about 3 bucks, plus some damn good pizza.

The place was a revelation. One night, I had to fire the chef on a busy Friday night. And guess who had to cook? Yours truly. But I really knew I was in business for myself when someone came to me with the disturbing news that the toilet was plugged up. Moments later, I realized the only way to effectively unblock it was to put down the plunger I was holding and, umm, reach my hand into the commode and unplug it myself. Welcome to the restaurant world, Romano!

The Gladiator concept went over well, and we built up a steady following. Unfortunately, my business partner turned out to be jerk. It wasn't long before the honeymoon soured. He was an Italian but not the kind of Italian I was. He had no people skills and a grating personality, and he seemed to have an inflated idea of his abilities. A restaurant partnership can be like a marriage: Sometimes you really don't know what a person is like until you "marry" them. And in this case, my partner was strutting around the place like he was better than the customer. Diners pick up on such attitude problems pretty quickly. Most importantly, all he was interested in was wringing out profit from the operation. It made me think of something that one of my professors said frequently: "Service is primary. Profit is secondary." I told my partner that my priority was customer service and giving patrons what they wanted, which I said would reap far bigger benefits in the long haul. He disagreed.

So after about six months, I told him, "Either buy me out or let me buy you out." Trouble was, I didn't have the financial wherewithal to back up such a move. As I fretted about what to do, my father came to me and said, "Son, I'll get you the money." I asked him where he was going to get it. He said, "I'll get a second mortgage on the house." The pressure was really on me now.

Not the sweet smell of success but the fear of failure was driving me. If I blew this, my parents were going to lose the house,

I thought. I pressed on. It took me about a year, but I paid him back—double. Thank God that my first wife, Libby, was a school-teacher and had a steady income we could rely on. The financial security she provided let me take chances. The Gladiator grossed about $50,000 the first year, a pretty good number, and easily bested that total the next few years, before I finally sold it in 1968. While I didn't make much on the deal, it was a launching point.

Next came the innovative Nag's Head Pub, an English-style bar and restaurant in West Palm, where I joined two other partners. The Nag's Head was where I set the stage for what would become a cornerstone of all my future concepts: truth in feeding. I would keep no secrets from customers about the preparation of their meals. The kitchen and open grill would henceforth be visible to patrons. The Nag's Head would be the first of what's now known in the industry as the "demonstration kitchen" or "open kitchen." I call it truth in feeding. The food manufacturing process holds a lot of excitement and trust building. Let's get it out in the open!

I set up the char-broiler in the middle of the dining room floor, and my customers suddenly found themselves in the middle of the action, watching the showmanship of their own dinners being cooked and marveling at the bustle of the chefs and the flames that were lighting up the room. No longer would they have to ask themselves, "What the hell is going on in the kitchen back there." Back there was now up here. To this day, I'm apprehensive when I go into a restaurant and can't see the kitchen. I wonder, "How are they treating my food? What are they afraid to show me? Is the place clean? Are the ingredients fresh? How are they treating my food? Who, or what, is preparing it?"

There's an old marketing slogan, "You sell the sizzle, not the steak." Well, I started selling both the sizzle and the steak at the Nag's Head. We were also among the very first restaurants in the nation to have a salad bar. This was back in 1968, mind you. At first, the all-you-can-eat salad concept was a bit of a jolt to my customers, but it didn't take them long to catch on. Recall that Steak & Ale was among the first chains to roll them out nationally. We also sold martinis by the pound. Of course, we had to limit the poundage with some people.

Nag's Head grossed $130,000 for the first five months of operation—not bad 37 years ago. We were also the first to charge $1.25 for a hamburger—unheard of at the time. In comparison, a regular McDonald's hamburger was 15 cents and a Quarter Pounder was 35 cents. But you often had to eat several of those to be satisfied. So I just made a better, bigger burger, using higher-quality meat, cooking it in front of the customer, and serving scalloped potatoes with it. People went crazy for it.

Another Nag's Head point of difference was our presale of personalized pewter beer tankards. Before we even opened, I had sold 1,500 mugs at $15 each. Folks could put their names and business numbers on them, and we'd hang them up in the pub so they could drink from their own mug when they came in. If they let us know they were coming, we'd cool their mug for them. It made people feel like they had partial ownership in the place, a recurring theme at several of my restaurants over the years. The promotion was an instant success because we had a built-in customer base when we opened.

And my partners? It was déjà vu. They were profit mongers, not innovators.

So the point came where my partners didn't like the way I operated and I didn't like the way they did their business. Again, it was a push-pull situation: They'd have to buy me out, or I would have to buy them out.

That's where a devoted regular, real estate developer Vance Brittle, stepped in. He often told me that he felt that Nag's Head was the hottest and greatest concept of its time. Aware of the growing dissent in our partnership, he met with me and said, "You know, Philip, if your partners want to be bought out,

I'll buy them out for you, and we'll build these all over the state and all over the country. This is such a great concept!"

He asked, "How much would you want for your one-third?" I paused for a minute and said, "Well, I'd probably have to get $50,000." He never flinched and said, "Okay, then we'll offer them $100,000 for their two-thirds of the operation. And if they accept that, then we will build more stores throughout the country that you will operate, holding one-third equity in each store, and I'll put the money up. If they don't accept, then you're going to have $50,000 in your pocket."

"Fine," I said.

So Brittle gave me a check for $100,000 and, in turn, I presented it to the other partners for their part of operation. I told them that if they wanted to buy my share of the place, they'd have to produce $50,000 of their own for me. They had about a week to make their decision and come up with the requisite financing. Apparently, one of their parents lent them the money, so they did, indeed, buy me out. I thought I was getting a hell of a deal. I was still basically a kid, and 50 grand was a lot of money. Plus, I had retained the right to build Nag's Head restaurants all over.

So then Brittle came to me and said, "Okay, why don't you throw your $50,000 into the company, and we'll start building. You'll still own one-third of it, and you'll get a management fee for working the various restaurants. And when it's time to build another one, you'll get more money, more fees, plus you'll still have one-third and you'll go far with it."

But I thought, hey, if I could create this for someone else, I could create this—or something far better—for myself. So I said no thanks, pocketed the money and gave Brittle the rollout option. But not much came of the Nag's Head rollout after that. My old partners only opened one other location. I didn't walk away rich, either, but I had begun to realize that people would pay me money for my ideas, and I'd have plenty more creations to come.

Thanks to my father, Sam Romano, I had those two early successes. There's no telling what direction my life would have headed without him or whether all those restaurants I created would have ever come to life.

# 4

# THE LIFE AND TIMES OF ROMANO'S 300

## F o o d   f o r   T h o u g h t

I don't predict the future; I imagine it. And my imagination has no bounds. Neither should yours.

It was 1969, a good era to be enjoying the $50,000 I made from the Nag's Head sale. But I couldn't sit still for long. I still can't. So I decided to open a fine dining restaurant in Palm Beach called Romano's 300. It was on the ground floor of a six-story building that had just started construction on Royal Palm Way. I worked out a good build-to-suit deal with the owner, who was happy to ink a ground-floor restaurant anchor tenant.

I resolved that Romano's 300 would be the finest place in town, but I'd need to serve booze. I lucked into a liquor license but paid an exorbitant sum, $30,000, because Florida had a limited number of licenses, and you had to buy one from an existing license holder. I got mine from the owner of a newly defunct place called the Red Lion. So I quickly put it to good use.

It would be at least a year before Romano's 300 would be finished, so I acquired a little building across the street from the new building for a bar to keep the liquor license alive, plus serve as a promotional hub for Romano's 300. It was a good move, as it turns out, because the building would go up very slowly and the completion of my fine dining restaurant would actually take a year and a half.

I fixed up and reopened the bar, calling it the Key Hole, because patrons had to have a key to open the gold lock on its front door. Yes, a key. I didn't want just anybody coming in there, after all. But I did send keys to all the professional people who wanted one initially. If they wanted keys for their secretaries or wives or girlfriends (or just two of the three), they could write down the addresses and I'd send them one.

The key-access entry, I theorized, would make customers feel like they were part of something special. Psychological ownership, as I've noted, is one of the main comforts people seek out when they go to a restaurant or bar. It gives them that sense of belonging and recognition that makes them a regular customer. It's a concept I've gotten down to a fine art today. The mayor of Dallas, in fact, forced me into opening such a private club later in my career, when she led a crusade to ban smoking in the city's restaurants and bars, a touchy subject I'll tackle later.

At the Key Hole, we had a TV camera at the front door and a monitor atop the bar. That way, everybody could see who was coming, and they could dash out the back if they had to. You can imagine the scenarios where this came in handy. We charged ladies only a quarter for drinks from 4:00 PM to 6:00 PM, so the place was just loaded with women. As a result, the guys were almost breaking down the door. We also had a copper-topped bar, where we'd offer to engrave a person's name for $15. The proceeds went into a big glass jar behind the bar for use by an unwed mother's charity.

As our little watering hole grabbed the imagination of the locals, we developed a long wait-list for new keys. People would practically beg to borrow "member" keys for a night out. Of course, there were other bars around, and we had our share of competition. But we held up well by restricting entry and creating perceived value in the process. We did things that made people talk about us. I was beginning to realize that there is no end to the ways you can create the feeling of belonging.

One night, a guy came to the Key Hole and said he wanted to do caricatures. He clearly did great work. He charged $25, including framing, and each portrait only took him about 20 minutes. I put him in the corner booth and said, "I want you to charge $50 if they take the portrait home and $25 if they hang it up in here. That's my only condition. You're welcome to work here anytime you want. And you can keep all the money for it."

He agreed, and before long, the place was a wall-to-wall portrait of patrons and their guests. On a typical night, a guy would approach the place and realize, "Well, here's my key to get in. Inside, I've got my portrait on the wall, and I've got my name on the bar." That's ownership and belonging times three!

That year, I made more than $50,000 and learned a few things, experimenting with different ideas and just having fun. But Romano's 300 was finally ready for occupancy, and I had to close the Key Hole to move my liquor license across the street. By that time, anticipation of the restaurant's opening had reached a peak.

We opened Romano's 300 in December of 1970. I got an SBA loan to open the place (it seems like I was one of the few people in this business at the time to pay back an SBA loan), and took on a partner, so I really didn't have to use any of my own money in this venture.

I had decided to make Romano's 300 a closed club at lunchtime and an open restaurant and bar for the general public at night. I sold memberships—about 300 of them—to men for $100 apiece just for those lunch privileges. Thus, the *300* in the restaurant's name. A lot of the early members were young businessmen who hadn't been able to get into the exclusive Everglades Club and other exclusive clubs in Palm Beach, so they were happy to fit in at my place, which had a dozen dining areas and a terrific basement wine cellar. The 4,700-square-foot place was my personal castle with a fantasy medieval English theme that drew a lot of attention.

At the time, no other place was convenient for some of these folks to conduct their business. I installed phones in various small dining rooms and provided pens, writing tablets, and other niceties for them.

We also did some unusual things for our members. I arranged for interesting and unusual people to come in and give presentations and speeches. But they weren't your typical toastmaster types. There were a couple of guys who came in and talked about Cuban cigars, wine people discussing fine wines, and call girls—yes, call girls—talking about how to treat a girl and how to know when you're getting hustled. And boy, the place was packed with people wanting this briefing. I got blasted in the paper for it, but the guys loved it, and the publicity generated even more interest.

We served complimentary hors d'oeuvres and champagne to customers awaiting tables. Every night, women would receive a complimentary rose and a little extra attention. Regulars quickly got their preferred drink delivered to the table without having to order it. The "guest" menus, by the way, did not have prices. Only the guys got the dollar-sign versions. (I don't think we could get away with this anymore.)

I had traveled throughout France, Spain, Portugal, and Morocco previously and studied European cuisine, which gave me some presentation ideas for Romano's 300. As a novelty, we had American, Italian, and French cuisine with prices listed in dollars, lire, and francs. Most of the recipes came from my mother, aunts, and uncles and had been in the family for a long time. My family had eaten this way when I was a kid.

There was a chef at the place named Pierre who really didn't get along with anyone, including me. He was an arrogant, American-bashing, pain-in-the-ass Frenchman with some talent but also a proclivity to burn more than his fair share of meals. I had brought him in for the season against my better judgment and he was being paid very well—too well in fact.

I called him into my office one day and asked him how much I was paying him. He answered, "About $25,000 per season, Monsieur Romano—you're very generous. Thank you!" So I said, "Well, I'll tell you what, Pierre, I'm gonna give you a raise to $40,000 for the season." He said, "Oh, thank you, thank you, Monsieur Romano! You are so generous."

But I knew—I just knew—that the S.O.B. would go back in the kitchen and brag about the raise to everyone. And he did. Well, the rest of my help thought I'd gone crazy, until about three days later when I called him in again.

I said, "Pierre, I'm really not too fond of your work—you're fired. Take your knives and get the hell out of my kitchen." He jumped up and said, "You are firing me? But Monsieur Romano, you just gave me a raise!" I said, "Pierre, I really don't like you. So if you're going to lose a job, I want you to lose a good one. See ya later."

Now, I don't know if I could get away with that today, either. In fact, it seems restaurant owners and managers don't have latitude to make such personnel decisions anymore. Most of them answer to human resource departments who answer to lawyers—two groups of people that know practically nothing about your business. The lesson learned here was that, while you can make a mistake in hiring someone, don't make the mistake of waiting too long to let them go. The problem will just get bigger and bigger. Too many managers and executives think that firing someone they've hired will make them look inept. In truth, keeping that person around to do even more damage reveals the manager as ineffective. And it also keeps somebody around who's probably going to piss off a key client or customer.

Of course, there'll always be that isolated problem that crops up no matter how well you plan. By the time I opened Romano's 300, I had learned that teaching my staff members how to handle an accident is almost as important as training them how to prevent it. A great recovery can create a loyal customer, because people will realize that you genuinely care about how they feel and that the one bad episode was an anomaly. They will even repeat their story to other potential customers about how you busted your tail to make things right for them.

My employees are taught to a fault that they have the ultimate responsibility for the customer service experience. The people they are serving have gone out of their way to spend their hard-earned money with us, and I remind them to never forget that. I have never been able to just shrug my shoulders when a customer has a bad experience. If you make 90 percent of the people happy, you will still have 10 percent who might not come back. Multiply that by a 1,000 customer visits and you have a 100 unhappy people, which is unacceptable.

I had 85 or so employees at Romano's 300. And though I'd brought in speakers for the lunch club members, I realized a couple of months into our operation that my staff could use a little enlightenment, too. I looked around for motivational speakers, but they all seemed lame.

So I brought in a local mystic—a peculiar but very intelligent little woman I'd met at a dinner party. She'd done a reading for me, and it went light years beyond the usual hokum. I was so impressed with her extraordinary perceptive abilities and her philosophies about positive thinking, synergy, and the "third eye," that I asked her if she could relate her talents to my business—more specifically, the success of my restaurant and its employees. That's when I first came to grasp the concept of visualization that, decades later, would become common not only in the mainstream business culture but in the professional sporting world as well.

When I told my staff what was going to happen, they looked at me like I had grown my own third eye. We assembled the wary staff in groups; managers, waiters, wine stewards, bellboys, and the like. She asked each of them to begin their workday with a three-minute visualization exercise where they'd imagine what they wanted to accomplish. The bookkeeper was to focus on piles of money and high cash balances. The maître d' was to envision large crowds and so much traffic that he had to refuse reservations. The chef would visualize smiling customers and rave reviews. And I would picture Romano's 300 winning all kinds of awards, publications writing front-page articles about us, and customers thinking about the restaurant constantly.

Hocus pocus or not, this positive-thinking pep talk seemed to pay off. The place was getting busier and busier, and the food was drawing better and broader notices as my people continued believing in themselves with the help of their daily visualizations. Not only did they no longer scoff at the notion, they were running with it, full speed ahead. To this day, people laugh when I tell them about the mystic. But she helped us see that the world was ours for the taking, if only we'd decide to see it that way.

Through this, I also realized that good things just don't happen by themselves, especially in the restaurant business. And I kept that in mind when I set out to win the prestigious *Holiday Magazine* award for Romano's 300. I talked to a dozen of my fraternity brothers and a few friends and said, "Do me a favor and write a letter to this food editor at *Holiday Magazine,* a Mr. Brazier, and get your friends and relatives to write letters as well. Mention the service, the scampi sauce, something else on the menu, and the wine selection—but make sure you write it in your own words so as to be believable."

There must have been daisy chain of about 100 people writing letters and it obviously worked, because one day I got a call from Brazier. He asked, "What are you doing, Romano? I'm getting twice as many calls and letters about you than about anyone else. In fact, I've never received as many letters about any single restaurant in my life."

I had to hold my hand over the speaker while I laughed. Then I got back on and said, "Why don't you come down, have dinner, and I'll show you?" He came and was suitably impressed.

Based on his visit and the merits of the dozens of letters, we came away with the *Holiday Magazine* award that year and in every successive year I owned the restaurant—a distinction that sure didn't hurt business.

Brazier eventually helped us get named as one of the top 175 restaurants in North America, and we continued to earn that distinction every year as well. I truly believe we deserved all of our press clippings and trophy case full of awards. The *Holiday Magazine* letter-writing campaign was just one illustration of how to make good things happen for yourself. The award binge continued—the Florida Trends Award, the Silver Spoon award, and others came to us. I couldn't help but feel as though my "third eye" was winking at the mystic whenever I was called on to pick up our mounting booty.

The lesson: A little aggressive self-promotion never hurts, as long as you've got the concept to back it up. The letter-writing campaign is just one illustration of how restaurant people can make good things happen for themselves. Sometimes, it's not enough to have great food, great service, and a charming setting. Some good old-fashioned song and dance and few well-placed calls to local media can go a long way. With all the chain restaurant competition today, good word-of-mouth and lots of publicity are essential for the independent owner.

Besides our strong local following, we hosted a lot of out-of-town and out-of-country visitors who had read about our food, outstanding service, and awards. One afternoon, a couple of very conspicuous, stern Jordanian men came in. It seemed that a very important dignitary was coming to town, and these guys were scoping out Romano's 300 as a venue for a dinner party for ten, to be held, at least tentatively, in a private room at my place three days from then. Before long, we figured out these guys were actually front men for royalty and the dignitary was none other than King Hussein himself. The men quietly acknowledged that fact, made us assure them that we'd act with discretion, and then started naming an elaborate list of exotic Lebanese food items they'd need to feed this regal entourage. I said, "Whoa, whoa. Gentlemen, I don't know if I can get this together. And even if I can, this could get very, very expensive and quite time consuming."

One of them—a reputed arms dealer whose name you'd recognize—said, "Listen, kid [I really was a kid back then], we don't care what it costs, as long as it's good and everything's perfect." I said, "Well, I think you just said the magic words. Hang on a second."

I got on the phone to my barber, who was Lebanese, and told him some of the items we'd need to find and prepare for a special dinner: there was stuffed lamb; a grape leaf dish stuffed with rice, parsley, and peas; kibbeh, which is raw, minced meat pureed with crushed wheat; and a lengthy list of other exotic items. He said, "Wow." He'd have to get back to me on this one. After a while, he did. "Tell him you'll do it," he said excitedly. "I got the ladies from my church, and they're going to prepare the whole meal for you."

We had three days to prepare a feast fit for a king. We even managed to locate some of the unusual wines they wanted. Everything was coming together. Apparently, the king had bragged to a friend and associate that he could go anywhere in the world and have the finest Lebanese cuisine put before him, and he was intent on testing his theory at my restaurant.

Among the organizers' many stipulations was that we couldn't take pictures of the king or his party. But my promotional mind was still abuzz. How could I capitalize on this potentially king-sized publicity bonanza? I remembered that the men hadn't said anything about photographing the meal or the preparers of the meal. So I called the food editor of the *Palm Beach Post-Times*, Rosa Tucca, and asked if she had ever seen a feast prepared for a king. I told her the story about King Hussein, the barber, and the ladies coming in from the church, and she just loved it. She spent the better part of three days hanging out in our kitchen and having a staff photographer take pictures of all the food and the women cooking it, all for a big spread in the *Post-Times*.

Before the dinner, a few U.S. Secret Service men came in to check things out. They got upset with me because the king's wine was sitting out in the open, breathing, saying it was an open invitation to tampering. I told them not to worry, that I'll sample each bottle myself before it was served. I did this as they watched. I didn't keel over. Various security guys also had to sample the food before it could be served. I helped them with that task, too.

And the fun continued through the night. After dinner, a couple of the king's people came up to me and asked if we could provide any "bubbly-bubbly." It took us a while to figure out that the king's people wanted to smoke some marijuana or hashish. So I went up to the Secret Service guy and asked him about the appropriateness of this rather unusual request. After all, this product wasn't exactly a staple at Romano's 300. He shrugged his shoulders and said it was okay with him, if that's what the king's entourage really wanted. I didn't think anybody was planning to bust King Hussein. One of our waiters, in fact, was happy to oblige him. He hurried home and quickly drove back to Romano's 300 with a bag full of "bubbly"—no questions asked. The group had its after-dinner "cocktail" after their departure, presumably.

When it came time to settle up, I approached the organizers with two bills in my pocket, one for $4,000, which was fair, and one for $7,000, which was also fair, when you consider it had been a highly successful meal that was truly fit for a king. I asked how everything was and they said, "Oh, perfect, just perfect. It couldn't have been better! The king loved it." So I took out the bill for $7,000. They asked if it included tax and tip, and I said, "The tax, yes, but not the gratuity." So they happily forked over another thousand-plus for the staff. I made sure my barber and the Lebanese cooks from the church were taken care of out of the tab, too.

The next day, I called my accountant at the time, a guy named Connie Gantz, to rib him a little bit. "Connie, I have some bad news and some good news for you," I said. "First, I served dinner to King Hussein last night." He said, "Aw, why did you go and do that?" He paused, and said, "Well, what's the good news?" I replied, "Well, I charged them over $8,000 for dinner, tax, and tip for ten people. Not bad, eh?" He shot back, "Gee, that's great, Phil. But you didn't take a check from them, did you?"

Anyway, we got a big splash in the paper, and Romano's 300 became known as "the Restaurant of Kings." And the king came back to visit us a few more times.

While Romano's 300 was still cranking full blast, I opened another place in Vero Beach, Florida, called Friends of Edinburgh Eating & Drinking Society, named after the capital of Scotland. Irish pubs were all over the place, so why not a Scottish pub? I had visited several during my travels to Scotland and had a few ideas of how to run an Americanized version.

We put together a booklet that was a combination menu and history of Scottish pubs, then sent thousands of them to a friend in Scotland who would in turn send them back to us with a Scottish address and postmark. That would give the menus an authentic touch. Using choice demographics and zip codes supplied by American Express, I mailed these elaborate menus to would-be customers, inviting them to attend one of several grand opening parties. The place took off like a rocket.

It seemed that the menus from the pub had become a local collectible and were disappearing quickly—about half of the original 2,000 vanished. At about the same time, meat prices were soaring at an alarming rate. So I engineered a promotion where anybody who came in with the old menu could order at the old price.

This was a way to take care of the locals, most of whom had pinched menus from the place. The tourists, however, had to pay the new-menu price. This also worked when we raised prices seasonally during the tourist rush. Regular customer: old menu, old price. Tourist and seasonal visitor: new menu, new price.

My partner in Friends of Edinburgh, Judd Kassuba, was the same guy who'd invested in Romano's 300, and he'd done so when I really needed some additional capital. Romano's 300 was the first big restaurant I had done. I was getting a little overextended making those SBA loan payments and knew I would need some help pretty damn quickly. So Judd, a regular customer and very successful local real estate developer, probably worth between $5 million and $10 million at the time, came to my rescue, taking me up on my offer to sell him 50 percent of Romano's 300 for $100,000—based in part on my assurances that I would farm the money back into the business.

Judd continued to make some big money in real estate and was doing well in both my ventures, but he later ran into serious problems over some failed deals when the economy faltered. He had to file Chapter 11 bankruptcy. In fact, he was part of one of the biggest bankruptcy filings on record at the time—about $150 million. But he came to me beforehand to tell me he was being forced into the action and was worried about how it would affect everything we were doing together. I said, "Judd, no problem. Do what you've got to do, and we'll see how it settles. If I have to start over again, so be it." As it turns out, we were able to keep our deals separate from the bankruptcy, and it didn't affect either restaurant, which was a lucky break. Of course, Judd had to divest himself of our partnerships. Years would pass before our next dealing.

Meanwhile, I was taking Friends of Edinburgh forward. I had realized by this point that I'm really just a marketing guy who just happens to be in the restaurant business. I'm also an incorrigible opportunist. And I had recognized that marketing opportunities exist in economic downtimes and in times of crisis, if I just use my imagination.

During the so-called meat crisis of 1973, there was a "meat shortage" in the United States, so I thought I would stage a boycott at Romano's 300. I wrote a letter to the paper saying that if my restaurant and others would take meat off the menu, there would be more meat on the marketplace for housewives and families. I also wrote a letter to the president, to Congress, and everyone else I could think of.

Articles were written about us in local and regional papers, and the story made it onto the AP and UPI wires, then got picked up around the world. I got coverage as far away as China and Japan. They were calling my place the "Eatery of the King." A legislator even gave a speech on the House floor mentioning my efforts. I made the Congressional Record.

Truth be told, I really only took meat off the menu for a couple of weeks or so. My customers we're starting to grumble. I thought, well, I had already gotten more publicity than any restaurateur could hope to buy with that stunt, and you've got to keep the customers happy. So the meat shortage was over at Romano's 300. But the promotions weren't. During the energy crisis a few years later, I offered people a 10 percent discount if patrons ordered their meat rare and got more free publicity. "Anything to help the cause," I told the papers.

I didn't hesitate to use these same promotional philosophies at many of my later restaurants. The mystic helped me believe that the world was mine for the taking, if only I'd make it so. So I did. Soon, that world would get a hell of a lot bigger.

# 5

# TWEAKING THE MENUS

**F** *o o d   f o r*   **T** *h o u g h t*

So often, problem solving is what restaurant life is all about,
especially in hard times. Clubs, organizations, associations,
and business groups are always looking for a free place
to meet, regardless of the economy. Why not a restaurant or
nightclub? The ways to fill such places are limited only by
their owner's or manager's imagination. A few phone calls and
a little research go a long way.

**F**or the most part, I have preferred to build restaurants, sell them off, and move on to a new concept instead of living with them forever—with a few exceptions. And in my mind, the time had come time to sell Romano's 300 and move on to new things. So I sold the place to a guy named Guido Gerosa, who would later rename it Chez Guido.

Oddly, the Palm Beach area had no exceptionally good seafood place, despite its proximity to the ocean. So I bought an old barbecue place just west of the city on Military Trail and set about renovating it to open Old Shuckers restaurant in 1974. I

originally wanted to call the place Mother Shuckers but grudg-
ingly bowed to political correctness. (The same went for a place
I'd later open called Nachomama's, which Brinker International bought and renamed Cozymel's.)

We fixed the place up to look like a New England-style seafood eatery and built an oyster bar, or "raw bar," in the back, a
companion to my trademark open kitchen toward the front.
We had huge clambakes and were the first to sell lobsters "by
the netful," as we called it. There were Rolls Royces and limos
pulling up and a regular cast of highbrow patrons coming to
see us, rubbing elbows with beachcomber types and a wide cross-
section of other folks.

We got our tag line, of all places, from a cab driver. He said,
"Just about everybody who gets in my cab asks me where they
can find a real good seafood place." A light came on. We would
call ourselves Shuckers: A Real Good Seafood Place. We were
the first to bring really large lobsters to town and had the big
clams and big shrimp also. We charged $15 for a "clam bake"
for two people, including corn on the cob and red-jacket potatoes. Sound familiar? Other places quickly picked up on my
cue. Today, you'll find that format at seafood eateries throughout the country. Imitation is the first sign of success, I say.

Shuckers was a very nice place, but it was way out in the
boonies and had to have its own septic tank. We had a drain
field, and the thing was always backflowing, so the bathrooms
clogged up with maddening frequency. A lot of people were
coming in from Palm Beach and I didn't want them to feel put
out by less-than-optimal facilities, so I put a sign up on the rest-
room doors: "I know the bathrooms are not the greatest in the
world, but you didn't come out here to use the bathrooms, did
you?" Our patrons somehow managed to rough it.

Shuckers was a slightly irreverent place, and we had shirts
made up that reflected the droll tone: "Keep on Shuckin'," "We
Kiss Your Bass," "Not Tonight, I Got a Haddock." It was here that
I learned to buy fish by the truckload. My cousin, an enterpris-

ing sort, was working for me at the time, and he went to whole-salers at first for our fresh inventory but soon started dealing directly with fishermen. The place did great business, but it was too big and clumsy. While it had plenty of pincers, it didn't have "legs," meaning it would be very difficult to roll out elsewhere. I kept operating it profitably for about two years before selling it to a foreign company that bought it with Swiss francs.

But I didn't stow the proceeds in a Swiss bank because, yes, I was moving on to something else, as has been my lifelong custom. Next on my dance card was the First National Bar & Grille in West Palm Beach. The Grille was located at the base of three towers called Forum III that housed 1,500 hungry office workers. My challenge there was to feed them all lunch, if need be, in the course of just a few hours. Before I opened the place, I knew it was going to be a madhouse. So I decided to put up a buffet, though with a timely twist.

I charged by the minute!

I didn't care what the office workers ate or how much they ate. All I cared about was how long they ate. They would enter and actually punch in when they started and punch out when they were finished. I charged about $5 for a half-hour and $2 for every ten minutes after that. That got them in and out in a hurry so others could be seated. They walked in and quickly moved through the buffet, which featured chicken, beef, meat loaf, salads, and the like, pulled up a chair, and feasted. Most, as you can imagine, made sure to finish in that half-hour, and of course, we didn't nick them if they went a few minutes over. The customers were aware of my seating constraints and most were happy to cooperate. This approach was certainly a little off the wall, but it worked. We turned tables quickly as a result. At night, I charged a little more and did so by the hour instead of half hour, offering more entrée-type items such as prime rib.

Charging by the minute was a unique solution to a unique problem. As in most industries, problem solving is what success is all about in the food service business.

On the other side of First National was a big bar that seated 300. At the time, I was trying to operate the bar and grill separately, which was harder than I realized. We had a big sound stage, an elaborate lighting system, and Las Vegas-style entertainment, including dancing girls, singers, and other acts.

To do this, I had formed a talent and production company with actor Burt Reynolds, who happened to be an old high school chum of mine. Burt was three years ahead of me, but he and I were in the same high school fraternity together, which helped make us more gentlemanly and kept us out of gangs. We were also both ex-jocks, which gave us a lot in common.

My venture with Burt was called First National Productions. Our plan was to take local singers and other talent and see if we could develop them and maybe open clubs in other parts of the country. Burt used to take his "slightly" older girlfriend, Dinah Shore, home with him on holidays, and Dinah and I became friends. Burt and I found a young singer who had a terrific voice and personality and lot of potential, we thought. We taped her and resolved that the next time Dinah was in town, we'd have dinner at my home, let her listen to the tapes, and get her professional opinion.

Dinah listened intently, then said: "Boys, she's good. But she's not going to make it. She sounds like every other singer out there. She's not distinctive. She has no point of difference in her voice." I repeated the term in my mind: *point of difference.* Yes, point of difference. The singer may have been out, but Dinah was right on key. What a perfect way to summarize what my restaurants—and any business for that matter—needed to stand out from the pack and thrive. Every concept I create will have several points of difference. Dinah sang and I listened. She put into simple words what my father was always driving at when he told me to stand out from the crowd. And that's what I'll tell my boy as he grows to be a man. Have a point of difference. I tell him to be a better human being and greater human being than everyone else.

Anyway, picking out talent was obviously not my forte. And besides, this wasn't New York or Las Vegas or Hollywood. It was Florida. So nothing really came of First National Productions. Besides, Burt and I would have other things to do with our lives, as you might have suspected. Plus, the damn Florida economy was on the fritz.

Still, I had a lease to fulfill, and I had to find a way to fill the club up in the evening. Problem solving knows no bounds, especially in tough times. So I organized a woman's club. That's right, a woman's club. I got five women, ranging from their mid-20s to mid-30s or so, together for a gratis dinner—an accountant, a hairdresser, a travel agent, an architect, and a phone company executive. At the meal, I told them, "You know, for a long time, men have been networking, organizing, doing business with each other in the Rotary or Kiwanis or the like, and they network and help each other out. Women generally don't do this. But just think what you could accomplish if you got, say, a hundred women together. None of your group would be out of a job. And in this economy, that's all the more important. We could form an organization here, and I could help get you perks like free checking, discounts at different stores, and such."

I said, "If you can get that many women together, you can have a social hour in my place every day and parties once a week, and some free food on me. Start mailing lists and party lists. Guys, by the way, will be dying to get on that list."

To the person, they said it sounded pretty darn good to them. So I asked them to bring at least five more women each to the next meeting, and they all brought about ten. We had dinner again, and I explained the deal. The next week, each of them brought another 10 or so, and by then we had about 300. I bought them all dinner again, gave my speech, and they were all excited about their newfound empowerment.

They named themselves The Lovers, the Fighters, and the Wild Horse Riders—a Ladies Club. And I was their social chair-

man. They had bylaws and special shirts and had to pony up
$25 apiece to join. Every day, there would be a cocktail hour
with 75 to 80 women in the bar, and they all got discounts. It was
a terrific environment, because we had nice women and nice
men coming in and a dress code to further weed out the un-
savory types. At the parties, we'd charge guys $5 to get in. The
club would pocket half of the cover charge. I set up a little buffet for the women. The place was packed all the time.

We threw a First National/Ladies Club Fourth of July beach
party with buffets and bands at the Holiday Inn in nearby Jupi-
ter, Florida, and estimated the crowd at 3,000—at $15 a head,
which included all the roasted pig and booze you could consume. We literally stopped traffic on the main highway, and the
state police had to come to unclog things.

If restaurants and nightclubs have consistently empty spaces
and vacant party rooms, the ways to fill them are limited only
by the imagination of their owners. Plenty of clubs, organizations, and business groups are looking for a free or inexpensive
place to meet. A Chamber of Commerce directory, some phone
calls, and a little research can go a long way.

In 1974, when First National was still in business, I opened
a place in Lake Worth, Florida, called the Pasta Palace. I put
Pasta Palace in the old Lake Worth Theatre, which had originally
opened in 1939. So we created "terraced seating" in league with
the layout and showed silent movies and serials on the screen
with an old-fashioned projector we inherited when we took the
place over.

At the front entrance, where the concession used to be, we
installed an Italian deli with take-out foods and a visible pasta
machine where people could see raviolis being churned out.
The kitchen and the bar were in the orchestra area along with
seating for those who wanted to be in front of the screen. We
used the former theater loge boxes as special dining areas for
those who wanted more privacy. The menu was on the side of
the projection screen and it flickered on and off with pictures

and prices. Every three minutes, you could see the whole menu. We even had a curtain made out of neon lights.

This was around the time when the economy was getting bad in Florida and the real estate industry had ground to a halt. But when that happened, I still did pretty well at my places. After all, people still had to eat and have a little fun once in a while. And hell, they were drinking because times were bad. Why not drink at my place?

I had made a habit of never putting any of my own cash into anything. The banks saw me as a good bet and kept trying to lend me money to do new things. I told myself that this economy was going to turn around and what the hell, maybe I'd just overextend myself a little here and there. If it did turn around, I'd be way ahead of everybody else. And if it didn't, I'd be in the same boat with everybody else.

I spent a lot of money. And, well, I did end up in the same boat with everybody, and we didn't quite make it back to shore. I had already closed the First National. I knew I wasn't going to stay in the area, so I liquidated everything and paid my bills and came out with about $100,000. Ironically, things got a lot better in Florida about six months later. As in other fields, timing is everything in the restaurant business. This move was predestination, I'm convinced. It was a failure that launched me in a new direction.

My best years—my salad days—were in front of me.

# 6

# TEXAS ON
# THE FRONT BURNER

### F o o d   f o r   T h o u g h t

Two guys were walking along each side of a narrow river and
suddenly found themselves within shouting distance of one another.
One guy yelled to the other, "Hey, how do you get to the other
side?" The other guy yelled back, "You are on the other side."

**A**fter selling almost everything
we owned, Libby and I got in our Mercedes and drove through
America to check out the lay of the land and the breadth of opportunities. We finally settled on Texas, the last bastion of free
enterprise, it seemed, and a state full of people with big ap-
petites who needed more good restaurants.

One of the things that attracted me to Texas at the time was
an ongoing change in liquor laws. Previously, people had to
bring their own bottle to a restaurant. Now, the laws were loos-
ening up, which I realized would create new opportunities for
restaurateurs—myself included. Only about 60,000 people had
lived in Palm Beach when I was there, so I was considered a big
splash in a small pool. But San Antonio had more than one million people, so I thought I could become at least a small splash

in a big pool. But I think I misestimated my potential impact when I first came to the Alamo City.

When I arrived, the financial backers of a San Antonio country club—an insurance company—were planning to take the place back, and company officials told me they'd give me a third ownership in it if I'd take over and improve the food and other aspects. But I checked it out and realized it was already being operated acceptably by a popular community figure. So I passed on the deal, mainly because I wasn't sure I could do things much better, and I didn't want to look like the "black hat" coming to town to throw the good guys out on their ears. However, while I was in town looking around, I spied an enormous number of opportunities. This market was much larger than what I had been accustomed to in Florida, plus it offered a lot more wide-open spaces with no swamps.

I knew I could do a restaurant better than anyone else in town. I also realized I should first get into the more mainstream "eating" business in Texas, not just the fine dining business. In Florida, where my focus was on fine dining, that would have been a step down. But nobody knew me in Texas, and I had no expectations to live up to other than my own. It was 1976, the Bicentennial year, and I had the spirit, all right, but it was a creative one.

First, I decided that San Antonio could use a Shuckers. So I teamed with a couple of my Florida partners to put one together, and things went very well. They wanted to build more, but I declined. As I noted, I didn't think it was a very mobile concept, anyway. Besides, I only owned 25 percent of this deal and wasn't going to work my hiney off to come away with a fourth of the action. So I quickly sold my interest to them, and the place lasted only about a year after that.

Enoch's, a private steak and fish house named after a Biblical character, was next on the menu—my tenth concept. At the time, San Francisco Steak House was the hottest meal ticket in town and was doing at least 300 dinners a night. But I wanted to create something a little more intimate, with better food and fewer meals. There was one big obstacle, however. I hadn't been in Texas for two years, which was then the requisite period to get a liquor license. I complained to officials at the Texas Alcoholic Beverage Commission, telling them I had never been arrested and had served my country. They told me a liquor license is a privilege, not an entitlement, and that the two-year period was the law. (To this day, Texas still has some of the screwiest liquor laws.)

But there was a way around the law. I found out that if I formed a corporation with someone who was at least a two-year resident, and that person owned the majority of stock in the corporation, then we could get a license. Luckily, I had befriended a well-connected city council member and insurance salesman named Gene Carnavan, and he agreed to be that person.

I soon familiarized Gene with the invitation-only idea I had successfully implemented at the Key Hole in Florida, and he supplied me with the names of 25 couples he thought would be delighted by such a place. I sent them invitations for a free steak dinner at a new and exclusive restaurant. They came and feasted on T-bone steak, prime rib, and fettuccini alfredo and loved it all. I told the group, "My friend and your friend, Gene Caravan, has brought the 50 of you in here tonight for a complimentary meal. And what I'd like to do is give you a key. I want it to be a nice place where we've got the right kind of people. So we are locking the front door, but your names are going to be on our Rolodex. If you want to make reservations, you can come in and eat any time you want and with anyone you want. But we won't let a group in unless one of them is on that Rolodex and has a key."

We then asked each of those couples to supply us with the names of another ten couples, and I sent letters to all of them, saying they were invited to be inaugural members of Enoch's. All of a sudden, these people found they were not only part of something exclusive and exciting, but they also had the power to bestow their good fortune on their friends and relatives. It gave a mystique to the place and made it a destination. And it gave people that important feeling of ownership. Pretty soon, I had a core group of 250 people coming into Enoch's as a result of these letters, and I'd get most them to add yet another 10 people each to the list. I was rapidly developing a sizable peer group where most of the people knew each other and were generally compatible. We eventually wound up with a very healthy customer base of about 10,000.

So Enoch's, a small but very classy steak house seating 75 to 80 in New York bistro fashion, was born in style. Its ornate bar, handmade by my craftsman father, Sam, ran along one full side. He and my mother had moved to Texas to be near me when he retired, but my father, just like his son, had to keep busy, so he set up an impressive woodworking shop and did a lot of nice artisan-quality finish-out work for Enoch's and some of my other restaurants.

Booths ran along one wall of Enoch's with tables down the middle. It had terra cotta floors, a long brass rail along the bar, and all-mahogany ceilings and walls. My sister, who also moved to San Antonio, came in to help, along with my first wife and my mother. At the time, so many big restaurants were serving 400 to 500 meals a night around town, a diner's odds of getting a good meal in that format were dwindling. People were getting tired of feeling like cattle. So as to not compromise service and quality, I just wanted to produce 100 to 125 meals a night with a relatively limited menu but do those to perfection.

I really didn't want a traditional menu. So I put the actual main attractions for the night—the various steaks, fish, and shrimp—on a tray menu carried by waiters. We'd go to the tables and say, "Here's our list of entrées for the night." (Ten years later, the famous Morton's Steak House chain used the same idea.) Everybody got a Caesar salad made fresh at the table by a server pushing a salad cart around the restaurant. The food was good, the price was right, the place was always packed, and our private patrons loved the intimate atmosphere.

By this time, I had learned a few operational tricks. Most of these came from just thinking practically. I had noticed that one of the long-running mysteries of operating a restaurant is the chronic disappearance of silverware. Managers of other restaurants would ask me, "Are people really stealing that many knives and forks?" I'd answer, "No, they're not. Just ask the linen company that cleans your tablecloths. They probably have a good selection." An unbelievable number of utensils, I had found, get wrapped up and tossed in the dirty laundry, usually when somebody's in a hurry. I caught on to this and even cut deals with these companies to acquire such utensils for my less formal eateries, where mix-and-match forks, knives, and spoons were an acceptable part of the presentation.

Another tactic: If one of my kitchens has a lot of dish breakage, I will put a sign up indicating how much each plate and glass that's broken costs to replace. If I'm getting $500 a month in breakage, I'll put a sign up offering a $150 bonus to be split among the bussers at the end of the month—that is, a $150 bonus minus everything they break. So now they are wasting their own money, not mine, and I'm saving $300 or $400 a month. They have ownership of the situation plus a way to make money by not wasting my money.

Anyway, there was a pretty savvy employee at Enoch's who I sent to bartending school. Because showmanship behind the bar had come into fashion, I wanted him to take things one step further and perform a few magic tricks between orders. So when I saw an ad for a place called the House of Magic, I informed him that I was taking him there for training. We walked into the place, and an extremely nice lady greeted us from behind the desk. There was something peculiar about this establishment. I told her, I'd like you to teach my friend tricks, and I'd like to enroll him in regular classes. I'd like to get him really good at it, so please show him the ropes," I said.

The woman had a befuddled look. She sure was dressed quite provocatively, I noticed. It took a few more minutes before

I realized we were in a house of prostitution, not magic, and the only "learning" he was going to get was a different sort of trick.

"Now that's one hell of a training program I'm paying for," I said. "You can stay and pay for your own tricks." We drove back to the restaurant, laughing our asses off. Needless to say, he got his schooling elsewhere.

A few doors down from Enoch's was a little bar. It was starting to deteriorate, and an undesirable element had started to drift in. I was worried that its clientele would start dragging us down. The owner just said he had to serve any customer who walked in the door. I realized there was only one way to clean up the place: buy it. So I acquired the owner's lease, fixed it up, and we did some unconventional things with the place, which we came to call Barclay's. Because Barclay's was so close, it served as a nice after-dinner complement to Enoch's.

This was 1978 and backgammon was hot at the time, so I established a backgammon club, to which I sold memberships at $100 apiece. I hawked about 1,500 of them, making $150,000 right off the top, along with a nice operating profit from the bar. Obviously, we were entertaining a much more upscale clientele than the old place. I sold my drinks for a good price, and we hosted a number of fun events, like a New Year's Eve party in the middle of summer, complete with black-tie and tails, which generated some local publicity.

It was at Barclay's that we utilized a concept called eye-level seating. The bar was in the middle of the place, and the wall seats were all set as high as the barstools. That way, everyone was eye level, so if you were walking by and someone was sitting at a table or the bar, you'd meet his or her glance. You could walk up and start talking to someone without having to bend down awkwardly. We also had a piano bar, bands, and backgammon tournaments and lessons. I even put a small library in the place, so it really didn't feel like you were in a bar.

I'd had pretty good run, all right. San Antonio was paying off, the 1970s were coming to a close, and both Barclay's and Enoch's were still running full throttle. But I got to thinking about my culinary destiny in the 1980s.

*C h a p t e r*

# 7

# THE NAME THAT
# HAMBURGERS MADE

## F o o d   f o r   T h o u g h t

Customers have to say "Wow!" when they walk in the door of one
of my restaurants—wow to the look and then wow to the food.
Otherwise, they won't come back. My eateries and culinary creations
must put a smile on people's faces. That Wow! Factor simply
has to be prevalent in every one.

I love Italian food. But I also love
Mexican food, Asian food, steaks, seafood, chicken, barbecue,
and just about any kind of food fit for consumption and just
about any way of cooking it. But as a kid, some of my fondest food
memories—apart from those of my mother's Italian kitchen—
were of the simple pleasures of biting into a juicy hamburger or
hot dog. Despite the huge variety of restaurants I've created,
featuring some of the best entrées and recipes in the world, if
I had to pick a last meal, it would be one of those two very American foods.

And here it was, in late 1979, and I was daydreaming about
hamburgers again. Almost by force of habit, I stopped for lunch
at a McDonald's. There I sat, eating the same Quarter Pounder,
in those same funky-bright surroundings with kids and moms

and Ronald McDonald flouncing around the place like it was a circus. The Quarter Pounder was always reliably good—McDonald's has thrived on consistency—but it was no different than the Quarter Pounder I'd had in college, except it was twice the price. That's a mortal sin in my book, to charge a lot more but not improve the product.

At the time, the sad fact was that McDonald's was probably the best of the national burger chains. Several knockoffs were coming along, but they offered no points of difference. (Insanity, I like to say, is doing the same things over and over and expecting different results.)

None of those prefab burger houses seemed to cater to a grown-up who wanted to linger over a freshly made meal, much less wash it down with a cold beer or two with a friend. In fact, the lighting, décor, and design of these joints was all designed for turnover—to get you in and out as fast as possible, unless you were there for a kid's birthday party.

My God, what an opportunity. I could create a more upscale burger place—a playground for adults. Surely, others like me were tired of these childish hamburger mills. In fact, having seen the sour faces of other solo adults in McDonald's over the years, I knew there was a niche. The hamburger is nothing new, of course, but some of the best creations in the world are variations on a theme, where a few imaginative twists take an idea to its next evolution. Enough marketing research. It was time to get busy.

So I started out with the challenge of how to make the "World's Greatest Hamburgers." My restaurant Bill of Rights— those things I hold sacred for every operation—was already starting to form in my head. I broke it down into six points:

1. *Meat.* It would be the best.
2. *Buns.* They would be the freshest.
3. *Cooking.* The burgers will be cooked exactly the way customers want them.

4. *Condiments.* Customers will be able to put whatever they like—and as much of what they like—on the burgers.
5. *Atmosphere.* The place would be exactly what customers expect from the home of the World's Greatest Hamburger.
6. *The people who execute it.* They will do all these things better and different than anyone in the industry.

And boy, did I have a name. Fuddruckers. I'll pick up later with the story of how I arrived at that. Meanwhile, I produced a rough floor plan, business plan, and mission statement. And most importantly, I fleshed out the six points of the Fuddruckers Bill of Rights:

1. *Meat.* We will grind our own meat, purchase beef by the quarter, debone it in-house, and use no additives. It will be grilled the day it is ground. It will never be frozen.
2. *Buns.* We will bake them freshly on the premises all day long. They will be hot to the touch when we give them to the customer.
3. *Cooking.* Our chefs will cook the burgers on black-iron griddles. They will cook them to customer specifications, first searing the meat and then cooking it to perfection. They will cook only the meat so that becomes their only focus. The buns and condiments will be handled separately.
4. *Condiments.* We will give the customers a perfect burger and a hot fresh bun. They will take it to a convenient, fully stocked condiment bar that will be so big and full of fresh vegetables that it resembles a produce stand in a supermarket. It will offer them everything they could possibly want to put on their burger and as much of it as they want.
5. *Atmosphere.* There will be truth in feeding, and we will put people in the middle of where the World's Greatest Hamburger is made. Everything will be prepared and cooked openly, including the ground meat. There will be a glassed-in butcher shop where the meat is visibly

ground. The walls will be lined with premium supplies and products, including bins of produce and cases of beer, ketchup, and mustard. There will be a separate, visible bakery where the buns are baked from scratch. Customers will smell the baking bread and will watch as bakers carry trays of hot buns across the dining floor to a serving area, yelling, "Hot buns, coming through." All these preparation areas will be clean and orderly.

6. *The people who execute it.* They will be youthful, energetic, and enthusiastic and will commit to doing their jobs better than anyone in the business.

It was now time to see my banker, Charles Cooney, about start-up money. I bet he'll love this idea, I thought. I had established a solid, professional relationship with Charles shortly after I got to town. He was a stand-up guy who had watched me pay off loans for Shuckers, Enoch's, and Barclay's religiously, then make healthy deposits into my personal bank account.

So I showed him the planning materials, explained my six-point plan, and said, "Charles, I really want to do this other restaurant that I'm going to call Fuddruckers, and I need $150,000." He carefully listened to the concept and how Americans needed a better burger and a relaxed setting to eat it in and enjoy a few cold brews. But he balked. "Phil, I'm going to play the Dutch uncle here and do you the favor of some tough advice. It's not going to work. I just don't like the idea. You've done well at fine dining. Why lose your focus? Forget about burgers and beer and stick to what you know."

I persisted a while, but he still declined. He just didn't want me to risk messing up my other deals. I said, "But Charles, I don't have any other bankers. You're the only one I've dealt with since I got to town. You've never let me down before. Where am I going to get this money?"

He said. "Trust me, I don't think anybody will give it to you for this . . . Fuddruckers thing."

I said, "Charles, I know what I'm talking about. This is a great idea. I'm still going to do it." He shrugged his shoulders and said, "Fine, but you're not going to get the money from me." I grumbled and couldn't help but think of the entrepreneur's definition of a bank: a place where they'll lend you money if you don't need it.

In fact, virtually all of my ideas for Fuddruckers—including the slightly naughty name—were scoffed at and called "unworkable" and "frivolous" by other financiers, restaurateurs, and assorted naysayers. I had long ago realized that the unconventional can be a tough sell in this business. Many an idea that is initially considered "unfit" for its nonconformity has gone on to rock the world. So it's often the case that the unfit, not the fittest, survive in my industry. I gathered from the way I was getting shot down that I must really be on to something.

So I devised my own private investment plan. I'd beat the bushes for ten good investors—perhaps hit up some of my well-to-do customers at Enoch's—who believed in me enough to put in $15,000 each. I'd give these guys 48 percent of the company cumulatively, while I retained control with 52 percent.

I threw my net out, gave away a lot of drinks and dinners, and came up with several dozen "provisionals," or guys who talked a big game but whom I knew might back out when it came down to brass tacks. The first to make a firm promise was Richard Signorelli, president of Friedrich Air Conditioning Company. In fact, when I explained my Truth in Feeding concept, my customers' Bill of Rights for the place, and my plans to make the world's best burger, he was ready to take a shot on the spot. "When these are opening up from coast to coast, as I envision them doing, you're gonna look pretty damn smart," I told him.

My critics told me there was no way in hell I was going to make this work. "What a hassle. What an expense. Poor yield. Pain in the ass. Waste of space. Butcher your own meat? Whatruckers?" You name it, they said it. But I was just stubborn enough to ignore them. I had already set out to solve the logistical problems these unique elements would present and weave everything together to create this concept.

From my past experiences with meat suppliers, I realized I could never be sure of the freshness of the product, what was in it, or how long ago it had been ground. But I figured out a way that my hamburger would cost me only 30 to 35 cents a pound and I could become my own quality-control expert.

The formula was actually quite simple. We'd buy each quarter, which weighed about 110 pounds, for about 95 cents per pound. We would debone them, and then I would take out the ribeye and cut it up to make about 13 to 15 pieces, which we'd use to make some very fresh ribeye steak sandwiches for about $5. So the yield on the ribeye would be a quick $70 because the steak sandwiches, I theorized, would sell briskly, which they did. I subtracted that $70 from my original cost. What remained was the expense of the 90 remaining pounds of hamburger left after the deboning. And that came to less than 35 cents per pound. People told me, "No way your ground beef is going to be that cheap. I'm paying $1.80 a pound." Well, do the math.

We'd not only do all our grinding, we'd do it in plain view of the customer. Truth in Feeding will prevail. I had promised at the onset of this program that I would take all the mystery out of the hamburger, and this approach is as demystifying as you can get.

I had already toured Fuddruckers dozens of time in my mind before we even had drawn up plans, much less found a location. I finally settled on a nice little building on Botts Lane near the San Antonio Airport—a former print shop—and got to work. My father, who made frequent appearances there and still had a discerning eye, took me aside one day and told me that my construction crew was "as slow as shoemakers, and they're not doing a very good job, son. Get 'em out of here. I'll build you this place myself." So I fired them, and we worked side by side for several weeks, a time I still treasure today. He was in his mid-60s, but the old man knew what he was doing. Hell, I'm 65 now, and I like to think I know what I'm doing.

I had hustled together nine investors but still had one unit left. One day, a distinguished-looking young businessman came in to check out Fuddruckers before it opened. I explained the concept, and he said, "God, this is a great idea. Do you need a partner?" I said, "No, but I have one investment unit left at $15,000. He bit. Three days later, I got his check. The guy was Herb Kelleher of Southwest Airlines fame. That said a mouthful about my idea.

Fuddruckers would have a simple menu: burgers, steak sandwiches, hot dogs, wurst, beans, fries, cookies, and ice cream. (Taco salads and chicken breast sandwiches would come later.) As noted in our Bill of Rights, we designed the place so that when customers came in, they'd see crates of fresh lettuce and tomatoes, cases of premium beer and ketchup, sacks of potatoes and sweet onions—all top quality. I called this functional décor. Customers would get a sense that our ingredients were the best around.

We started putting together our team. To me, the hiring process is a little like a casting call. I look for passion and a willingness to fill a role with creativity. I look to see what applicants have done with their lives, if they've shown the ability to go to school and buckle down and study. I try to determine if they have a respect for their family and for themselves. What they look like physically is often telling. If they don't care about themselves, how could they care about anything else, much less my restaurant? During the hiring process, I make it clear that I demand total effort. I like to hire young, energetic people with passion and desire. Often, it's hard to teach an old dog new tricks, though there are exceptions. Most of the kids, though, already have the basic smarts. I can always teach them wisdom.

I instructed our bakers to yell things such as, "Careful, hot buns coming through, out of the way!" It was a maneuver designed to call attention to the unique freshness of the buns—part of the shtick, part of the show. I wanted to put my customers out in the middle of the making of the World's Greatest Hamburger, where they could see all the products that went into it and on it—and all the beer cases lined up.

On our first day, my mother walked in, saw all the dry goods on the floor, and said, "Oh my God, you're not ready to open yet! Is this the back door or the front door?" I assured her this was how the place was supposed to look.

We invited about 50 friends for lunch as a test. The Wow Factor was immediately evident and seemed to be growing exponentially every time the next few people walked in the door. Person after person looked around and went, "Wow!" More wows followed on their first stop at the condiment bar and, of course, their first taste of a Fuddruckers burger. "It looks like a hit, Phil," they'd say, rubbing their bellies. "I'll let you know in six months," I always responded. In the restaurant business, you are only as good as your last meal.

We'd custom-cook our burgers on a black-iron griddle to taste—medium well, well done, you name it. "After all, it's your burger, not ours," we said. Even when we were busy, we would never mash the patty to speed the cooking time. People could see their food being prepared every step of the way. Truth in Feeding prevailed. We had just two burger sizes when I founded the place. The large was a healthy half pound. Keeping in mind the McDonald's Quarter Pounder faux pas, I actually added an ounce to my big burger after a while just to make it better, but I didn't hike the price.

I'm often asked how I arrived at the name Fuddruckers. Well, my answer all depends on who's asking. Fuddruckers was conceived in the late 1970s. So I either say I was inspired by smoking good pot with friends or by drinking good whiskey with friends. Some say when you twist around the word *mud-fucker* enough times, substitute a *fudd* here and add an *r* there, then you have it. But I really wanted to come up with a name that everybody was going to remember, and it had to be off-the-wall funny. And Fuddruckers, based on people's amused reactions, stuck. It had a funky, familiar ring to people, but it wasn't really offensive in itself. I even concocted an elaborate, tongue-in-cheek tale about our "founder," Sir Frederick Fuddruckers, and sold limited-edition prints, T-shirts, and Mother Fuddruckers mustard at the restaurant.

Politically correct, we weren't. In fact, I never have been. Crowd pleasing is my game, not conforming.

Fuddruckers was a one of a kind, too. The experience became a unique, personal one for the customer. We were the first to offer them unlimited toppings. They could go to the produce area and heap them on, ladling up as much free melted cheese as they wanted from our crocks. They took ownership of the process. We even had a couple of very attractive shoe-shine girls at our first Fuddruckers. We were also among the first restaurants to give people free drink refills.

It was a smash. We had a second location in Houston open within a year. Several franchise locations would follow. Fuddruckers was sprouting wings, just as I envisioned. We tried to locate in areas with a high density of apartment dwellers, because these were customers without traditional backyards, and we wanted to become their backyard. We became both a physical and emotional extension of the lives these patrons had when they were growing up but couldn't access now. We had covered patios so people could eat outside in nice weather. We were one of the first restaurants to offer buckets of beer on ice. We became a comfortable place to hang out with family and friends.

Because I'm both a marketer and showman at heart, I'm always thinking about novel ways to promote my businesses. The letter-writing campaign to *Holiday Magazine* for Romano's 300 was an inspiration for another promotional push at Fuddruckers. Only this time, the campaign would be national in scope, as we started to roll out our restaurants around the country.

Because I felt I was serving the world's greatest hamburgers, I was intent on being recognized for it. To expedite the process,

I made up my own organization, the Hamburger Appreciation Society of North America (HASNA), called up a good friend in Minneapolis, and asked him to become its figurehead president.

Not surprisingly, HASNA had a Best Hamburgers contest. And guess who won? That perennial champion, Fuddruckers! It always looks good to have awards on the wall, and because no one was giving out awards for burgers, I had to establish one myself. Somebody asked, "Isn't that illegal?" I replied, "Hell, why would it be?"

A restaurant can have great products, but the best one, perhaps, may be the products of its owners' and managers' imaginations.

After a while, my semifictitious HASNA president was getting letters from people all over the country asking how to join the organization and telling him how great Fuddruckers burgers were. Every time we went into a city, we got a list of American Express card users and sent them a letter from HASNA telling them that the award-winning hamburger place, Fuddruckers, was coming to town and that they accepted American Express cards. (Remember, I had used a similar tactic at Friends of Edinburgh.) The HASNA promotions sold a hell of a lot of burgers.

I've never been afraid to take a creative tack in selling my concepts, even if my means seem to border on the outrageous. Creative opportunities in businesses are boundless. But they seem to be limited to just a handful of individuals in the restaurant industry. Think of how many times you hear people say, "Well, you can't reinvent the wheel." To that, I reply, "If the wheel was never created, maybe we'd be getting around faster with something better."

There's a norm out there, and everybody kind of stays within it and conforms. If you're too systematized in your development approach, everybody's going to be doing things the same way. Creativity is stymied. You let the system think for you. It's like the guy who's driving along and spots two city workers laboring on a median. One is digging a hole, while the other is shoveling the dirt back in the same hole. The motorist stops their car, jumps out, and says, "Hey, I'm a taxpayer, and it seems to me you're wasting taxpayer money with this operation." One of the city workers responds, "We'll, we're a team of three. We plant trees, but the guy with the tree is not here today."

It's unfortunate, because systematized thinking makes it very hard for someone to break out of the box or kill the sacred cow— or even display it, like we did at Fuddruckers.

The HASNA thing at Fuddruckers was definitely not a by-the-book promotion. While it got us a lot of attention, that funky Fuddruckers name was even more of an eye-opener for the public.

A little later in our evolution, we were forced to sue several Fuddruckers knock-offs, including B.R. Others, Purdy's, and the publicly traded Flakey Jake's, for copying us. In the case of B.R. Others, a doctor in San Antonio had apparently been to the original Fuddruckers and then joined with his brother to produce a Fuddruckers clone in the Phoenix area—hence the B.R. Others name. The brothers apparently liked the concept so much that their floor plan, tile, chairs, walk-in cooler, and a number of other elements were exactly the same as Fuddruckers's.

In court, I was accused by the opposition attorney of giving my hamburger chain a name that would be easy to mispronounce as an obscenity. An attorney for the opposition got up and started interrogating me about how we came up with the name. I said, "Well, I thought it was unusual and unique and people would remember it."

The attorney replied, "Now tell the truth, Mr. Romano. It was meant to form something dirty or obscene in people's minds, wasn't it?" I said, "No, I don't think so, unless you do. And if you do, then you've got a problem." The jury was amused, and the judge chuckled. Shortly after that, my lawyer got up and started questioning me. He said, "Mr. Romano, when you started Fuck-rucker's . . ." The jury practically rolled with laughter this time, and so did the judge as well as everybody else in the courtroom. I fired back, "Hey, who are you working for here, them or me?"

We actually lost that case, but we won on appeal. It was among one of the first decisions involving "trade dress" in restaurants, and we were establishing case law. *Trade dress* is what a restaurant looks like, its theme, its design, its color, its music, its smell—even its quirks and funny little nuances. It is the feeling the place gives you—a kind of sensory psychology. But it's also a distinctive energy that has been created, and it's an energy that can be protected.

We sued these companies and filed injunctions barring them from building more restaurants until the case was resolved. That held everybody at bay while we went out and built the heck out of Fuddruckers, both establishing and protecting our market penetration. In doing so, we were able to put some real teeth in trade dress.

It quickly became evident that I couldn't protect a restaurant's functionality. Anybody could grind their meat in-house, make a Fuddruckers-style hamburger, and get away with it. It was tough to stop imitators from making burgers that tasted like mine or were made like mine. But I could stop them from making their place look like mine. If a customer comes into a restaurant and thinks, "Wow, this looks like a Fuddruckers and feels like a Fuddruckers—and I guess that's what brought me in here," then the operator directly violated my trade dress rights by setting things up that way.

It's like Campbell's soup. If I had a label that looked exactly like a Campbell's soup label, with the same design and the same typeface—only I had named it Smith Soup or Romano Soup—it would confuse shoppers. As a result, they might throw my soup in their baskets. But I'd be stealing an asset that Campbell's spent a lot of time and money developing—the design scheme, the look, the advertising, and the secondary meaning of warmth and comfort it conveys to the public.

Trade dress is also the way you guard a concept's exclusivity, like the way McDonald's fiercely protects its famous golden arches and its proprietary look, feel, and layout. If you see golden arches somewhere, you expect it to be affiliated with McDonald's in some way. Essentially, a trade dress violation is when somebody has come up with a product or concept that clearly usurps someone else's operation. That holds true with a restaurant. At Fuddruckers, I spent a lot of money to have my walk-in coolers walled in with glass so customers could see our people cutting the beef. I didn't have to do it that way, but I did it specifically to create a signature look and spent a bundle in the process. People who did the same thing with the same approach in essence took my assets and capitalized on them. It's the same as thievery. You want to be able to protect the concept once you've invented it. After all, you've put a lot of effort, talent, and sweat into it.

I've always said that imitation is the first sign of success— not just the sincerest form of flattery. But there were just far too many remarkable similarities to Fuddruckers in these establishments, and they seemed to be cropping up all over the place. People would come to us all the time saying, "Ya know, Phil, I was out of town and walked into a place that looked just like yours, down to the display kitchen and the colors and everything. In fact, I thought it was a Fuddruckers."

So I got a lawyer named Rocky Schwartz with a major Dallas law firm, then called Aiken-Gump, to help me go after these imitators one by one. We won every case straight away after that first victory on appeal over B.R. Others

All those places had to alter their copycat appearances, because the courts found that if a concept creates confusion in the marketplace, then it must be changed. Their glassed walk-ins would have to be covered up. The open bakeries with the fresh buns would have to be moved to the back. They couldn't use the kind of white tile I used. They could use green or red or blue or any other color. The message was starting to ring clear to the restaurant industry.

Today, I continue to get calls all the time on trade dress and have appeared as an expert witness in a number of cases. In fact, I was one of the first people to really put some teeth in it. I was an expert witness for Hard Rock Café when it sued Planet Hollywood for infringement of trade dress. My testimony essentially was, "Hey, they both look the same." Hard Rock Café won, settled, and got their just due. There is obviously very little difference in the two concepts except that Planet Hollywood displays movie memorabilia instead of rock memorabilia. Who's fooling anybody?

I was also an expert witness for Taco Cabana when Two Pesos copied them. They not only got Two Pesos to change everything they did, they nailed them for millions of dollars in damages. Two Pesos had entered Taco Cabana markets, conspicuously using the Taco Cabana look and concept and just beating them over the head with it. (In today's legal world, I would have received monetary damages from my lawsuits as well.) It became obvious that Two Pesos had flagrantly copied Taco Cabana's restaurant layout and interior designs. Taco Cabana took over Two Pesos after the U.S. Supreme Court finally settled the legal battle in their favor.

I spent a lot of time on airplanes and in court through the years for the sake of the restaurant industry. But it's been worth it.

While Fuddruckers was suing imitators, it was kicking into high gear and expanding. Because of the demands on my time, I had to sell off Barclay's and Enoch's to two different investors. Enoch's, incidentally, lasted about five years, but Barclay's continued to operate as a pub until the late 1990s.

A year and a half after its founding at that little Botts Lane location, I was prepping Fuddruckers for an initial public offering. Just when I had the world on string, my father took ill. It was cancer, it was spreading quickly, and he was going downhill pretty fast. We still hung out together as much as his health allowed, and he even attended board meetings with me. Once, he fell asleep right next to me in the middle of some bombast from a board member. I was getting a little drowsy myself. To this day, if a meeting lasts too long, digresses from its purpose, or gets too boring, I just get up and walk out. Sometimes people make the mistake of thinking I'm going to come back.

A little earlier in my Fuddruckers career, another influential man in my life, the guy who launched the hugely successful Steak & Ale and Chili's chains, entered the picture. I only say "entered the picture," because this man—Norman Brinker of Dallas-based Brinker International—was more or less pushed right out of it.

Rosalie, my sister, was working at Fuddruckers at the time, and when Norman came in and gave his business card to her, she told him, for some reason, that I rarely returned phone calls. So Norman yanked his business card back and put it in his pocket. I'm sure he was more than a little pissed off. Rosalie didn't tell me about his visit for a while. I finally heard about it some time later, but I still didn't make the move to contact him. For a decade, he did his thing and I did my thing. But Norman would reemerge in a big way later, and we would become fast friends and business partners.

Fuddruckers enjoyed a wildly successful initial public stock offering in 1983. We opened at $7 a share and soared to $18 a share that first day. The IPO has often been compared to the Boston Chicken IPO of a decade later. Boston Chicken, now Boston Market, burst onto the public scene in November of 1993 with a concept focusing on home-style chicken meals and fresh-cooked veggies that became known as "home-meal replacement." Later, I would come up with my own idea that would take home-meal replacement to the next generation and feature "restaurant-meal replacement." Boston Market afforded baby boomer professionals and other people who were too busy to cook the opportunity to pick up a home-meal quality dinner on their way home. That stock took off from $10 to $23 its first trading day and soared to $41.50 before later taking a free fall for a variety of reasons. (How many days in a row can you eat chicken?)

Fuddruckers had a successful secondary offering eight months later, and by the end of 1984, we had grown to 25 company-owned stores and 30 franchise units. We grew the chain quickly and not without some criticism from stock analysts. But sometimes rapid growth is the only way to protect yourself in a business where imitators—and lawyers—would love to get their mitts on your market share.

My father became increasingly ill, however, and I was heartbroken. When he was on his deathbed, I told him, "I'm so sorry, dad. I'm just at a point now where everything is going to pop." He said, "Don't worry about it, son. Think about me when you're doing this, and I'll be there." My father died at the age of 72 with me at his side holding his hand. While he didn't live to see most of my successes, I didn't experience the overwhelming sense of loss so many people feel at such moments, because I had been able to spend a wealth of time with him, had no regrets in our relationship, and felt no lingering issues or guilt. I never had to say, "Oh my God, it's too late," or, "Gee, I sure wish I would have done this with him." Our relationship had been strong. He was a good role model. We were both at peace. And to this day, I feel his presence in whatever I do. I know he'd be proud of what I accomplished. I was very proud of him. If my son has even half as much respect for me as I had for him, I will die a happy man.

But life went on. Fuddruckers continued with the unconventional promotions. We had the *Fuddruckers Burgereater's Review* every month. We'd produce capsule movie reviews in a Movie Menu section, rating features from one to three burgers, and we put the publication in all of our restaurants. I estimate we gave out 700,000 of them. The customer could voice opinions in it and pass along jokes in a section called "Laughing Stock." There was a record review section and a Pro and Con page where we'd invite politicians and other people to debate hot issues in what was a kind of community forum. We did this through the mid-1980s, and it was extremely popular.

We also had a scholarship program in place. Students had to take a minimum amount of hours to be eligible to work for us part-time. Of course, we were glad to see our employees make As and Bs in college, but our main concern was that they made the grade at work.

We would also take a percentage of sales from a particular store and apply it to a scholarship. So the better our people treated the customers and the harder they worked, the more gross sales we would have. The kids would all vote to see who would get scholarships at each store.

The monies generated would range from $2,000 to $4,000 per unit, and we'd spread them out among three to five workers per store to defray the cost of books and other expenses. I gave buttons to these kids that said, "Because of you, our customer, I'm going to college." I also ran promotions saying, "Not only are you getting a great burger, you're helping put a kid through college." The program gave people a little added impetus to spend their dollars at Fuddruckers.

We put together a Fuddruckers University (some of us called it good ol' F.U.), where managers and prospective managers underwent an exhaustive six-week program, featuring a butcher shop, bakery, and grill. Candidates had to quarter a side of beef and come up with the correct yield before winning their certification.

My bonus program for Fuddruckers managers was also novel. I'd give them each $10,000 bonuses at the beginning of the year instead of the end. But I would put that money in an account for them that wasn't accessible until the year was over. Every time we'd have missing hamburger inventory, we'd deduct from the $10,000. "The money is all yours," I would tell them up front. "But we will deduct what you lose." Just like the bussers who were given an end-of-month bonus, minus their breakage, Fuddruckers managers were spending their own money instead of mine.

Meanwhile, Fuddruckers continued to enjoy successful growth. But all of a sudden, I found myself getting claustrophobic. I was earning around $500,000 a year, plus perks, but I still had the feeling that I was being held captive. I couldn't do new things or new projects. I had grown tired of dealing with Realtors, bankers, underwriters, accountants, lawyers, public relations people—tired of just about everybody except the people to whom I could relate best: the folks who ate at my restaurants.

I wanted to do different concepts, but I couldn't, because the investors who had put their money in Fuddruckers wanted me to build a bunch more. So I said, "Hey, we have the company in good shape, and I want to step out of this thing. I'll sit on the board, but I'll turn things over to my executive vice president, who's doing a good job and who is quite capable. I'll still oversee things a bit. But I still want to be able to do things I want to do. And if you don't want me doing these things while I'm sitting on the board, then I'll get out." They said, "No, no. We still want you on the board."

In 1986, I sold my majority interest in the company. Fuddruckers merged with Boston-based Daka Restaurants, and its headquarters were later moved to Beantown. Eventually, the company was spun off to form Unique Casual Restaurants. Unique Casual sold it for $43 million in November 1998 to King Cannon, Inc.

The best part of the Fuddruckers story is that the guys who had enough faith in me and my concept and anted up the $15,000, made about $3.4 million apiece when we went public, all in less than two years. They didn't have to put more money into it during that time, nor did they have to assume any liabilities. They made out like banditos.

Some businesspeople in San Antonio still talk today about Fuddruckers as the one that got away—that one big chance they had to make their fortune. "I shouldadidit," they say. To this day, when I'm seeking investors, I tell them, "Don't be a shoulda-didit." I bought out one poor guy early on for what he had paid in because he acted like a total jerk. He was sick to his stomach when he found out what happened.

But Herb Kelleher, a man known for making many good business decisions, had cashed his share out early, after I informed investors that I was going to take a chance and expand Fuddruckers. He still made a nifty little profit, but nothing close to $3.4 million. I guess Herb did all right for himself without Fuddruckers, but every time I see him, he says something about that missed opportunity. He knows he should have flown round-trip with me—I would even have served the in-flight meal. But Herb knows airlines. I know restaurants.

Another investor friend of mine, Judd Kassuba, the real estate guy who was part of a $150 million bankruptcy back in Florida and who partnered with me in Romano's 300 and Friends of Edinburgh, had stayed in touch with me over the years. When Fuddruckers was going public, we talked, and it was obvious Judd was still struggling. He felt a few select deals would set things right again for him. So I said, "Judd, you helped me out when I needed it, and I'll help you out now when you need it. You were my partner then, and as far as I'm concerned, you are my partner now."

I'll never forget what he did for me. If he hadn't helped me out when I was struggling to pay back my SBA loan for Romano's 300, I might not have made it to where I was in the industry. So I paid him back in spades. I gave him one million shares of stock, which was trading at about $17 per share at the time. People thought I was crazy for doing it, but in my book, it was the right thing to do. That was $17 million in return for the $100,000 that he gave me back in Florida to pull me out of the fire. So he got a big project going, leveraged himself, the stock went down a little bit, and he ended up losing everything. Well I was a little bit upset with him, to say the least. Fortunately, I had kept the vote on the stock, so when the bank took it, I had what the value was on the stock.

Fuddruckers was an absolute machine, and I stayed active with the chain, serving the company's board for another three years. I had even become a common sight in Fuddruckers kitchens during that span. But it became increasingly obvious that the people who took it over didn't understand it. They were compromising its principles, its Bill of Rights. They took away, or muted, many of my original points of difference.

Now, if you go into a Fuddruckers, they're not grinding the meat. They said they had to address some "practical concerns." Surveys said that 12 percent of Fuddruckers customers were turned off by seeing the meat being freshly cut. "What do you mean?" I asked. "If that 12 percent didn't like it, what were they doing back in the restaurant in the first place? And what about the other 80-plus percent who did like it?"

Regardless, the operations guys felt it would be a lot easier if that meat-grinding element was just whacked out. I said, "But that would also be cutting out the quality and showmanship that really launched this concept." I got the feeling I was talking to myself.

Then the bean counters came in. We had $8,000 worth of inventory on the floor—all this flour and ketchup and beer and stuff. Multiply that by the hundred stores across the country and, well, that's tying up $800,000 in inventory, they said. So they took that away and put in more tables to fill the space. But they didn't fill the tables.

Fuddruckers ownership had a board meeting six months later. People didn't like the new look, it seemed. The board's solution: "We'd better put in different colors."

How much would that cost? $30,000 per store! So I said, "Before you go and do that, why don't you go back to the inventory-on-the-floor concept and all the other things that got us to where we were in the first place? It would be cheaper." I got a few polite smiles and that did-somebody-say-something? treatment. They saw lost profit.

In 1985, I started distancing myself from the company and began selling my remaining stock in a deliberate, orderly manner.

And the "new" Fuddruckers continues to deviate from the original concept. Now, they bake the buns in the morning and just forget about them. That not only robs the place of some of the showmanship but it also creates waste, because they're often stuck with a lot of buns at the end of a slow day. Previously, we just cooked the buns fresh as needed. Plus, they've complicated the menu with the addition of a lot of new items. They've hidden the bakery equipment and the butcher shop area. A window display with just a few ground-meat patties is all that remains of what I thought was a crucial Truth in Feeding element. Like so many other chains, Fuddruckers is trying to be a TGI Friday's or a Chili's. It's supposed to be a burger joint.

In fact, I got a call a few years ago from British entrepreneur Michael Cannon, one of the ownership partners of Fuddruckers's current owner King Cannon, and he asked how I thought Fuddruckers could be restored to its original luster. I said I'd be glad to help them take it private, fix it, and then take it public again. I'd done it before. But I never did hear back from him.

Do I get upset when I go into a Fuddruckers today? Yes. They have compromised the original Fuddruckers Bill of Rights. But they still have a damn good hamburger and I wish them success.

Besides, I got about $17 million out of my Fuddruckers stock deal eventually, so that made it a little easier to walk away back in the 1980s. Fuddruckers was my twelfth restaurant concept, but I was hardly content to rest on my laurels. There would be many more innovations to come. I got to thinking about all the things I've done in my life that people told me I'd never be able to do, including Fuddruckers, and how I wouldn't be where I was if I listened to them. And to this day, I laugh when I recall how one food reviewer called the first Fuddruckers a "poorly located, dime-store-decorated burger joint." In 2005, there were about 200 of these "joints" around the world.

# 8

# OPENING A VEIN
# AND STRIKING AN ARTERY

**F** *o o d   f o r*   **T** *h o u g h t*

Throughout my life, I've often been asked why I don't do things by
the book. Well, it's because "the book" is for people who aren't
creative enough to figure out a better way.

**R**estaurants are both my hobby
and profession, as I often say. And Fuddruckers left me with a
nice little nest egg. But I saw no reason to sink all of it back into
the industry or, for that matter, bury it in the financial markets
or the bank. So I thought about investing in other people's ideas.
If I could come up with good ideas, I should be able to recognize good ideas.

As I learned from my Fuddruckers experience, plenty of
people out there have potentially lucrative and revolutionary
ideas but are being shot down by formula-driven lenders. So I
decided to become a venture capitalist—an investment "angel"—
and take a few carefully measured risks.

As a venture capitalist, I'd have to see two things before
I would invest in someone's idea: a distinct concept and that
person's ability to execute it. I saw those very things in pair of

enterprising San Antonio physicians. The first of them, Dr. Richard Schatz, I met at a dinner party at the Dominion Country Club. He told me about a radiologist he worked with at the University of Texas Health Science Center in San Antonio. Schatz's partner, Dr. Julio Palmaz, had invented a miniature stainless steel implant called a stent that, when used in a balloon angioplasty, would help keep open coronary arteries prone to clogging. The device, originally called the Palmaz-Schatz Stent, was essentially a small, expandable tube of wire mesh. The doctors were convinced that it could be used throughout the arterial system in a variety of medical procedures.

They told me that the University of Texas system had run out of patience with them and decided not to fund their research on the stent anymore. The school's patent committee turned down Julio's request for a patent filing on it because they just couldn't see the value in it. A request for a federal grant to assist in developing the device was also nixed. So they asked me if I would be interested in investing in their invention.

I was intrigued and went to look at it. I listened carefully to the two doctors, whose acute dedication to the idea and its potential impact on the field of medicine seemed remarkable. While I had turned down other entrepreneurs seeking help, this device really piqued my curiosity. My gut instinct told me that if this nifty little invention reached the marketplace, it could hugely benefit both the population and the future of medical research—plus be quite profitable ultimately.

But this risky field holds no guarantees, and the slightest snag could set us back years, I thought. I showed the project proposal to my accountants and my attorneys, and they all said, "No, don't do it. It's got to go through the FDA, and it's going to cost a lot of money and take a lot of time." While they actually saw merit in this product, they just didn't like the idea of my tying up my money in it. I did it anyway. I liked the two doctors and I liked the idea. I thought the marketplace held a great need for it.

In addition to the good gut feeling I had about this, I also respected the two doctors and had the utmost confidence in their ability to take it to the next level. So I committed $250,000 to a company we formed called EGP (Expandable Graph Partnership) for further research and development, in return for a 30 percent partnership. The doctors would now have time to work some of the bugs out of the prototype, and I would handle the business end of the partnership, including the marketing strategy and all the negotiations with the different companies when the time came to sell the idea.

Before long, we had something impressive to show to the medical community. The industry was certainly wide-eyed when we started shopping around the world's first stent. The various medical products reps could barely contain their enthusiasm for it. Within a year, we sold it to a Johnson & Johnson subsidiary called Ethicon for $10 million plus a lucrative 17-year royalty stream—before the stent even received FDA approval!

Today, our group—the two physicians and me—has garnered about a half billion dollars in royalty checks from that paper-thin device. For me, that was roughly a $165 million return on a $250,000 investment. Johnson & Johnson has since said it was the most successful medical device they have ever produced. Sure, I was at the right place at the right time with the right people and the right product. But more importantly, I had the resolve to take the risk and ignore my advisors.

Some cynics may note that I'm playing both sides—getting people's arteries clogged up with my cheeseburgers and rich entrées and then treating them with the stent. Well, they're entitled to their opinions. I could go on about how I've always offered heart-healthy options at my restaurants, even before that term came into vogue. But I'll just say I'm proud to have bankrolled the stent, for everybody's sake. Today, I hear from friends who have one. And I start thinking, what if I'd never gotten behind these doctors and their invention? Would these friends even be around to give me the latest medical update? A former dinner guest and neighbor of mine, Vice President Dick Cheney, has one. Mother Theresa had one. Hell, I may need one myself someday.

After we sold the stent to Johnson & Johnson, Julio and I cofounded another medical company in San Antonio called Applied Bio Prosthetic Surfaces (ABPS), headed by the more-than-capable Christopher Banas, a nanotechnology expert. We also sold Johnson & Johnson the technology that will allow them to crosspollinate about five of their patents. They paid us almost three times as much up front for this company as the original stent deal, along with a sizable royalty agreement. In 2004, by the way, ABPS had about a dozen issued patents for technology that it had produced, with at least five others pending or in various stages of R&D.

About the time I was financing the original stent, I also formed DocuCon, an image-processing company involved in another revolutionary technological venture. I partnered with the former chief executive officer of Datapoint Corporation, Edward Gistaro. DocuCon specialized in setting up systems to convert paper files into automated retrieval data. Edward, a technological genius, served as CEO, and in 1987, we won a $9.2 million contract with the U.S. Navy to convert documents to optical disks. The technology has evolved now, but in the 1980s it was pretty damned edgy, or so I came to understand. (I am not a high-tech guy.) The company went public in May of 1989, raising $3.2 million in its IPO. I stepped aside as chairman in late 1989 and turned it over to Ed, who was the brains of the operation, but I remained a director of the company for a while.

The stent landed me on the cover of *Inc.* magazine in September of 1989, alongside a billionaire named H. Ross Perot, in an article headlined, "Who's Really Financing America's Start-ups?" The spread prompted my mother to ask, "Who is this Ross Perot fellow on the cover with you?" I said, "No, mom, I'm on the cover with Ross Perot." Today, ironically, I live two doors down from Ross in the Preston Hollow area of Dallas.

Though I have a high profile in the business world, I've never been a corporate kind of guy. I don't fit the mold, nor have I aspired to fit the mold. At one point in my career, I was doing a number of joint ventures with a major company, and the owner brought in an industrial psychologist to do some expensive testing on his high-level people. The owner told me, "Phil, it's costing me about $20,000 a shot to test these people. I've got an extra slot. Would you take it? You do a lot of projects with me, and I want to figure out what makes you tick. It might even be fun and you could learn something about yourself."

I didn't hesitate. "Sure," I said. "And I'll let you be privy to my results because you do a lot of business with me. But I also want to see the results of yours, because I do a lot of business with you."

Fair enough, he said. So the psychologist spent the better part of a week with me. We'd talk and have dinner, and he'd see how I operated with the company. When he was done, he said one evening, "I want you to take a test tomorrow." He came in the next morning, put the test on my desk, then apparently waited around a minute or two. But I never looked up, even as he left.

He came in a little later and asked if I was done. I replied, "Yep, I've been done a while." He picked up the test and soon disappeared. About two months later he returned to tell me about myself. The results were broken up into five parts. The first was "intellect." He said, "You know, this is the first time this has happened to me. I gave you the test and you didn't ask me any questions—what kind of test it is or how long it's going to take." He added, "And when I looked at the test, you'd done maybe half of it. The other stuff you left alone."

I nodded, and asked him, "How did I do on the ones I answered?"

"You didn't miss a one," he said. "Well, I didn't know the answers to those others so I didn't do them," I explained.

"That's what I thought," he said. He went on to grade me as "high superior" in intelligence in the first part of the test, based largely on my selective approach. This is always how I operate: solve only the problems that you have an aptitude for. If I need something done out of my area of expertise, then I just find somebody who's an expert to do it. I don't practice law or accounting or try to self-medicate.

The second part of the test was motivation. What motivates me is problems, he said. Indeed, I like problem solving. That's what stimulates me when I'm creating. He said that I abound with creativity.

Third was a segment on self-perception and how others perceived you. He said I was right on track with both. A true jerk, I've said, is a guy who perceives himself as the greatest guy in the world while everybody else perceives him as a jerk. In fact, there's a story about a guy who's seeing a psychiatrist. "Doc, doc, everybody hates me," he said. The doc said, "Nonsense. That can't be. You haven't met everybody yet." Another problem person is the guy who doesn't think he's worth a crap but everybody thinks he's talented and great. (I'd rather work with the latter than the former.) The psychologist said I knew what I was and who I was, and everybody perceived me the same way. I had a lot of respect for other people, and other people had a lot of respect for me, he said.

The fourth category was how I was using myself in my organization and whether my organization was structured properly. I don't do things by the standard pyramid organizational chart, with the reporting lines dropping down straight from the chairman and CEO. "True, I never do things by the book," I said. "'The book' is for people who can't figure out a better way."

While I was taking the test, I thought about a joke about two guys, John and Joe, who were applying for a corporate job in the human resources department of a big restaurant chain. The HR director said the one who gets the highest mark gets the job. When they were done, she held up the two tests and said, "John, it looks like you got the job." But Joe says, "Hey, I got a 90 on mine, just like John." The HR director responds,

"Yes, you did, Joe. But John put 'I don't know the answer,' as a response to #10. You wrote, 'I don't know the answer, either.'"

Well, it was my eye for someone else's creativity that helped bring the world its first medical stent. In 2003, the latest in a series of stent technology breakthroughs came with Johnson & Johnson's release of the drug-eluting stent named CYPHER. This stent delivers drugs that greatly reduce rates of restenosis, which is a renarrowing of the artery at the site where a stent is used.

In early 2005, close to a million coronary interventions involving the stent have been done. *In Vivo* magazine called it "arguably the most important medical device launched in the last two decades." It's also been named as one of the top ten patents that have changed the world. The first FDA-approved stent has even been on display at the Smithsonian Institute.

I have continued to partner with Julio, whose day job is chief of cardiovascular and interventional radiology at the University of Texas Health Science Center, and we're working on several new medical patents. I tell people that I'm in the restaurant business because I love it, but my fortune was really made by investing in ideas other than my own. The future would hold more medical ventures and problems to help solve.

# 9

# FAILURES AND DISAPPOINTMENTS (PART I)

## F *o o d   f o r*  T *h o u g h t*

Sometimes an entrepreneur's goals are a little different than
the reality he finds once the doors finally open. It's like the kid
who came home from school one day and told his dad he was
confused about something. "Dad, we're studying theory and reality
and having a tough time telling the difference between the two."
His dad said, "I'm a lawyer, son, and I can help. Go ask your mom
if she would sleep with somebody for $2 million." The kid
reports back to his dad, "She said she would." The dad said, "Now
go ask your sister the same thing." The kid comes back and says,
"She said she would, too." So the lawyer replies, "There's your
lesson, son. In theory, we are worth $4 million. In reality,
we're living with a couple of prostitutes."

**P**eople are quick to say that
everything that I touch turns to gold. "Wrong," I tell them. "It
turns to hard work." Sometimes, it turns to red ink. If you're in
the restaurant business long enough, try enough different concepts, form enough partnerships, and deal with enough
lenders, you will fail at some point. With so many moving parts,
it's just a given that something will go terribly wrong. While it's

crucial that you know when to throw in the towel, it's more important that you come away with something—a takeout—from that failure. One thing I learned was this: To be a successful entrepreneur in the restaurant business, you must have the stomach to take risks. Risk very much corresponds to reward. And in the business of starting concepts, you've got to be able to afford to close them.

Though the 1980s were good to me, I still suffered my share of failures and learned more lessons in the process. There's a saying, "There's no use running if you're on the wrong road."

## STIX EATING SPA

With the growing public awareness of good nutrition and international food, the timing seemed right in 1985 to put together a healthy Asian restaurant. So I opened one in San Antonio in January of 1986, a pan-Asian concept with Yakitori cooking. Stix Eating Spa was inspired in part by my travels through Asia. Stix, named after the kebabs we sold, fit nicely into a compact, 3,300-square-foot little building that seated 125. It had a theater configuration with high ceilings and banked rows of stadium-style seats overlooking the bustle of a central exhibition kitchen. People ordered meals from glass display cases and they were served by fast-moving staff wearing running shoes.

Our charbroilers were narrow and very long, and the cooks worked with surgical precision in front of everyone. All the activity seemed to enhance the notion that patrons were getting fresh, nutritious, healthy food. We had great meat skewers, stir-fried dishes, and salads and imaginative takeout boxes. The food was served in different-sized compartmentalized containers, similar to Japanese bento boxes. There was no smoking in the place and no hard liquor but a large selection of beer and wine.

However, we were only doing about $60,000 a month, when we needed to average $100,000. I started spending $25,000 a month on promotions on the radio and elsewhere to jump-start things but saw only negligible changes in sales. What's wrong with this picture, I wondered? You're supposed to get your money back plus at least a 10 percent return on an advertising investment. So I hired a market research firm to give me some answers. The good news was that my diners loved the place—I had 100 percent acceptance of the food and theme. In fact, patrons were even coming into the place more frequently than customers return to fast-food places, which is quite an accomplishment. The bad news: I was only attracting an upper-crust clientele, the $65,000-a-year family, which was high end for the times. The real bad news: only 6,000 of those families lived in all of San Antonio.

Stix price points were by no means exclusive, but the latest nutritional information had simply not filtered down to other potential customers. It wasn't blue-collar stuff. More people were starting to think thin, but they were still eating fat. It was a great concept but not the right place. It would have thrived in New York, Boston, Chicago, or Los Angeles but not in San Antonio. Still, I wasn't about to move Stix, or myself, out of town, at least at that point in my life. So I took videos of the operation and zipped it up a year after I opened it, losing $1.2 million on the deal. I had learned an important lesson: Cutting-edge ideas usually work best in densely populated urban areas. This notion would come in handy several years later.

## BARONI'S ITALIAN CLOTHIERS

After dropping out of the top post at Fuddruckers, I indulged myself in a lifelong dream to open a clothing store. As a kid, I'd walk past a place called the Auburn Pants Factory with my buddies, and we'd look through the window at all these designer clothes that none of us could afford. In 1986, I partnered with Philip Marky to open Baroni's, a high-end men's Italian clothier in San Antonio that was to be the first in a chain. Marky knew the business, and I invested not only in the business but in him.

We had beautiful suits and clothing made of imported fabrics, and we catered to an affluent clientele. A tailor worked in the outside display window for all to see, and we had an attractive female barber who gave free haircuts and manicures to our customers. The people who patronized us looked terrific from head to toe when they left the place. We opened up six stores altogether, including locations in Houston, Austin, and San Antonio, but the chain lasted less than two years. Again, we had the right idea in the wrong place. Our demographic was just too narrow. My Baroni's losses totaled more than $700,000. In effect, I got a couple of $100,000 ties and a $500,000 suit out of the deal, I'd tell people after we folded, because that's what this venture cost me.

## TEXAS TORTILLA FACTORY

In the late 1980s, I took a look at the New York City market and felt that its time-strapped residents could use some quick, tasty, portable Mexican food. So in the summer of 1989, I launched my plan to open a chain of taco restaurants in the Big Apple, partnering with Arthur "Christy" Powers, an old high school chum who lived in New York at the time. In doing this, I'd have an opportunity to try something I'd always wanted to try: Create a restaurant chain funded by penny stocks. A New York company did an initial public offering, or IPO, for us and we raised $600,000 in penny stocks for the debut of the Texas Tortilla Factory. We had the option to raise an additional $3 million to open new stores if we exercised our warrants.

Our first Texas Tortilla Factory store went into the bustling Wall Street area and did a brisk business. It featured visible black-iron rotating grills and tortillas made from scratch. The freshly made soft tacos were served in buckets, similar to movie popcorn containers, and came in several "Texas-style" varieties: beef fajita, chicken fajita, bean-and-cheese, sausage-and-egg, etc. Each item cost less than a buck and could be eaten on the go or at tables and stands just outside our "factory."

At the time, a small chain of four or five little Mexican restaurants of about 1,200 square feet each, called Peso's Mexican Food, was in town, and it was struggling. So I offered the owner stock in my public company to merge his locations with my fledgling business. It might save him, I thought, and it might save me capital because I wouldn't have to build each taco restaurant from scratch.

My idea was to promote these taco stands by giving every patron a free share of stock, instead of a free taco, as a grand-opening plug. I'd have all my New York patrons owning shares of stock, and they'd feel more than just an emotional or sentimental attachment to the place. They'd have a real ownership in the business and an incentive to return. But for logistical reasons, that idea would have been hard to execute, we soon discovered. So we figured out a way to give a customer "rights" every time they bought food, and if they accumulated 100 certificates during the first 6 months after the restaurant's August opening, they could trade them in for 100 shares of Texas Tortilla penny stocks. I'd post the stock price next to the menu specials each day and place company news and financial press releases on every table.

However, we brought that idea to my underwriters, and they told me I couldn't do it because of Securities and Exchange Commission regulatory concerns.

I told them I didn't understand, because here I was, trying to give the average consumer something back when big-time stock players were being indicted for stealing from them. *Inc.* magazine picked up on the controversy and wrote an article about it, photographing me on a street corner in Times Square handing out shares of stock. Nevertheless, the promotion died before it was born.

But the Wall Street stand was still hot stuff. We started working on our second location, and I went back to the same underwriters to exercise my options to convert the rest of the Peso's sites to Texas Tortilla Factory stands. But there was an even bigger problem this time. The underwriters had gone belly up. Our second round of financing literally disappeared. So we just buttoned up the business, and it was history. It worked, but it didn't make sense for me to put a pile of my money into a public company. So goodbye taco stands and goodbye New York, at least for now. I'd be back later, however.

These ventures were risky, like all new concepts, but they didn't fail for want of quality products. Of course, risk is relative. I tell myself that I possess the confidence, ability, passion, and creativity to accomplish my objectives, so it's not really a risk. But even if you have a creative flair, your ideas won't work without adequate financing and an underlying discipline of practicality. There are no guarantees in any business, particularly the restaurant business, no matter who you are.

Sometimes, as with Stix, you can get even a little ahead of your market. Stix was created about 20 years before this book was written, or about a decade before its time would truly come. Some of my favorite restaurant chains, P.F. Chang's, Pei-Wei Asian Diner, and Brinker's Big Bowl, are taking pan-Asian to new heights these days.

After Stix went under, I thought I'd go dormant for a while. So I decided to build a nice home in The Dominion area of San Antonio and realized that, as a hands-on guy, I wanted to take part in constructing it. I went to the site every day and really got involved working with the crew. I hammered and sawed and moved brick for the two years it took to build the $2.3 million home. It was a way I could feel like the place was really mine. I found myself wishing my father was around, so he could tell me how I was doing and, more importantly, how the construction crew was doing.

But I didn't feel as though I was using my true talent. (There's a lot of that going around.) There's a tale, in fact, about an underchallenged chief executive who finds a magic lantern, brings it back to his office, rubs it, and is granted two wishes by a genie. His first wish is to be whisked off to a beach and be surrounded by beautiful women who cater to his every whim. Zap, he's seaside with a bevy of beauties. The genie asks, "What's your second wish?" The guy pauses and says, "I wish I could sit on my ass all day, just do nothing, and never have to work." Zap, he's a CEO again, back in his office.

Well, my office is in my mind, and secretly, I was burning the midnight oil in my brain, just dying to conjure up something more constructive to do.

# 10

# PHILVILLE'S FAMOUS GRILL— I CALLED IT MACARONI

**F** *o o d   f o r*   **T** *h o u g h t*

What's the top ingredient in a successful restaurant? It's not
location, location, location. It's food, food, food.

**S**ometimes, restaurants far off
the beaten path thrive for six decades and restaurants in the
greatest locations in the world shut down in six months. That's
puzzling to some, but it's not a mystery to me. If I had a choice
between a great location and a great concept, I'd take the concept any day. In fact, I've long held that if you could put a restaurant in the middle of nowhere and serve outstanding food,
people would find it.

I had a rare chance to prove that theory. My new San Antonio house sat on a high elevation, and I had a great view of
the sprawling "hill country" from my picture window. On clear
days, I could see a small town off in the distance called Leon
Springs. A very old burg, it was less than ten miles from San Antonio and was little more than a jog in the road near Interstate
10 West. One day, I decided to drive out and inspect the town.
There, I noticed five or six nice-looking little stone buildings
sprawled out on about five acres along Boerne Stage Road. A

few of them even housed decent little businesses. I returned several times, and each time I did, I noticed more and more traffic was flowing through the town.

This was late 1987, and the springs, after which Spanish explorer Alonso De Leon the Younger had named the town, had long stopped flowing. But something about the place got my mind percolating. There was an abandoned hardware store that at one time had been a dancehall, and I couldn't help but think what a nice restaurant building it could make. There was also a grocery store/gas station called Rudolph's that, I found through a few friendly inquiries, did around $400,000 annually. Another decent-sized place, a two-story former restaurant building, had once had a brothel operating on the upper level. Nice little buildings, nice little town. Maybe I should buy the whole place, I thought, before laughing at the notion.

But maybe it's not such a whimsical idea after all, I reasoned. I had been mulling over a few restaurant-concept ideas, and this might be just the "laboratory" to test them. I just happened to know the guy who owned all the commercial property in the town. He was a Realtor and an investor, and one day I finally asked how much he wanted for the whole place—and I mean the whole place. We dickered back and forth, and I ended up paying him about $600,000, though I think he had his heart set on a bigger sum. I knew that buying the whole town would help insulate me from having to deal with inspectors, zoning, excess regulation, and all those little headaches.

At the time, the economy was dragging in San Antonio, and a lot of businesses were going bankrupt. While I was reasonably sure that people would drive all the way out to Leon Springs just for my food, there were no guarantees. So I hedged my big bet a little mentally. "Well, I just want a decent place to dine," I told myself. "If people come or don't come, then fine." I still hadn't lost that healthy fear of failure, despite my successes.

My first concept in Leon Springs, as I've noted, arose in part from an unfulfilling visit to the popular yet pedestrian Olive

Garden. At the time, Olive Garden was the only national Italian chain. Italian restaurants were still mostly mom-and-pop shops. But I would create a hybrid concept that the world had yet to see, smell, and taste, and I'd put it in that spacious stone dance-hall building. Not including the purchase of the town, I put $150,000 into the place, including $100,000 into a wholesale renovation of the antique 5,000-square-foot structure, which featured massive stone walls, a giant fireplace, and exposed rafters.

I would name the place Romano's Macaroni Grill. When I was growing up, everybody in our little Italian enclave used the term *macaroni* for pasta, regardless of its shape or variety. It was all "macaroni" in a generic sense. Macaroni Grill's format really had its roots, not only in my upbringing as a first-generation American Italian, but in my grandparents' Sicilian home. As I've mentioned, the dinner table of my youth—we didn't have a dining room, so we ate in the kitchen—was a festive place, where family and friends shared wine, song, and spectacular food.

We set out to create an environment where people felt they were eating in an Italian kitchen. I'd noticed over the years that, at most parties, everybody seems to end up in the kitchen watching the meal prepared. So the visible kitchen, I felt, incorporated the patron into the restaurant from the start. It also helps put my chefs and other workers on notice that they have to keep it clean and that they have to look sharp in the process. Thus, we placed the kitchen at Macaroni Grill on both sides where the customers walked in.

Like at home, we'd put fresh flowers and a jug of wine, much like my grandfather had made, on each table and let people drink it in tumblers instead of wine glasses. And what the hell, I decided, customers could just pay for the table wine on the honor system. This drew skepticism from colleagues, accountants, and others. I told Alan Dreeben, one of the higher-ups at my San Antonio liquor distributor, Block Distributing, about the idea. He said, "That's crazy. The jug is too heavy. They don't want to drink jug wine," and so on. I was not deterred.

Incidentally, my attorney and good friend, Cecil Shanker, said he didn't like the Macaroni Grill idea, let alone the wine deal, but he sure got behind that failed Baroni's clothing store concept. For a while there, if Cecil liked something, I was afraid to do it!

Anyway, I just believed this honor system wine thing would make people feel a little more at home and maybe let them think they were beating the system if they happened to fudge on their consumption a little bit. "Just let us know how many glasses of wine you had when it's time to pay," we'd say on our menus. "You trusted us to cook your food; we trust you to tell us how many glasses of wine you had." Truth be told, we made a huge profit margin on the table wine concept, any way you measure it. And I saw it as part of the schtick.

We opened in April of 1988, serving about 1,500 meals our first full week. My mother and my wife were on hand to help as well as my sister, Rosalie, and other relatives. We were actually trying to build up to a full house slowly, but it wasn't to be. Business was so brisk on Saturday that we literally ran out of food, and we had to close early the next day. We did about 30 percent more business than expected.

Right after we opened, we went to the Italian-American Club, and the head of it was able to get all the Italian ladies together to come out for lunch at the Macaroni Grill. They got all dressed up, I fed them for free, and then we asked them to come outside and pose for a picture. There must have been 50 of them standing outside the restaurant in their Sunday best. We used the shot in one of our ads, identified them as Italian-American Club members, and said, "That's Italian! They can't be wrong." The image was quite effective.

Macaroni Grill featured grilled meats, fresh vegetables, gourmet pizzas made with fresh tomato sauce, and other Northern Italian fare. Ironically, my mother didn't really like the cuisine at Macaroni Grill when we first opened. But when we added some of her own recipes, she changed her tone.

There was an elevated entrance, so when people walked in the place, they were above everything. They could see all the people and the cooking activity on each side of them. They'd see informal elements, like the Christmas-style light bulbs that we strung along the entire ceiling, and think, "Well, this is inexpensive and kind of fun." Then they'd see the tablecloths and think, "Oh, it's going to be a nice place." But then they'd look at the concrete floor and think, "Oh, it is an inexpensive place, after all." Then they'd see the flowers on the table and think, "Or maybe it's more formal," and then they'd see the jugs of wine and think, "or less formal." It really put people on a roller-coaster ride, and it helped take the intimidation factor right out of the situation. The place appealed to just about everyone. People entering for the first time wanted to get down into that group of happy people and have a good time. The restaurant was a stage.

Refrigerators in the ramped entryway displayed meat and fish to patrons. Counters in the dining area displayed the special dishes and salads, while others were loaded with appetizers, desserts, and condiments. Just like in the old Romano family kitchen, diners munched on Italian bread that they dipped in olive oil and fresh-ground pepper as they waited for their food. And we employed real chefs—not just cooks.

The wait staff wore aprons and ties and worked from counters in the center of the room. Tables came equipped with crayons, and we encouraged patrons to doodle on the butcher paper we used for tablecloths as they waited for their food. Servers were taught to write their names upside down so amused patrons could read them.

Over the years, I had come to think of my restaurants as theaters instead of just places to serve food. The restaurant building is the stage, the customers and the staff are the cast, and the food is both the star of the story and its theme. All the elements of my creation had to act in concert with one another, down to the tiniest detail. There was interplay, action, color, sound, surprises, dramatic entries, exits, emotion, and much more at Macaroni Grill.

Well, Macaroni Grill was a smash by any definition of the word. People came in droves. We could seat 200 or so in our converted dance hall, but on weekends, we still had consistent hour-and-a-half waits. Once people had made the drive out there, walked into the place, and smelled the food, they weren't about to go home on an empty stomach. They were a captive audience. To ease their wait, I greeted them personally with gallon jugs of free wine, telling them I was grateful they were there.

And we didn't disappoint, serving up huge portions at medium prices. By comparison, Fuddruckers took almost a year before earning the recognition it deserved and generating as much traffic. Success took Macaroni Grill only a few weeks.

For most restaurants, Mondays and Tuesdays are slow, and after that initial onslaught, we were no exception. Advertising in the paper just created even longer waits on the weekends. So I concocted a crazy scheme, seemingly, where dinner would be free for everyone one Monday or Tuesday a month. The trick was, customers didn't know which day it would be. When you think about it, they really only had a one-in-eight chance of having a free meal. We rigged the telephones so nobody could call out to tip off other parties on freebie night, and cell phones were virtually unheard of then.

On the first night we did it, people had no idea it was going to happen. When they asked for the check, I gave them a letter instead. It said: "I am in the restaurant business. I really love the restaurant business. The only thing I don't like is having to give you the bill. So one night of the month, either a Monday or Tuesday, I'm really going to enjoy myself and won't charge anybody anything."

I told them that, if they liked the place and atmosphere and the food, please tell other people about it, because I think a restaurant should be talked about, not advertised. "I'd rather make you fat than the newspapers," I said. And I told them to be especially generous with the servers.

People went absolutely crazy. They couldn't believe it. Some of them cried. One guy came in with a party of 13 and didn't know what the hell was happening. He literally danced a jig when he found out. Some said they just couldn't accept what we were doing and insisted on paying. But we wouldn't let them, so they'd leave tremendously generous tips instead.

The guy with the party of 13 came back to me several weeks later and said, "If you think your idea didn't work, you're wrong. Every one of those people in my party has come back here with their families and brought other customers in, too. That was one of the greatest things that ever happened to us at a restaurant."

Crazy and costly? Well, I calculated it cost me about $1,500 the first night I tried the promotion, and based upon the $5,000 in business we did that evening but did not bill, I figured it was a bargain. To do a general promotion campaign like that in the media, it would have cost me $25,000 a month. I got away for $1,500. To get the idea to work even better, I got someone to take the letter to the newspaper and tell them he'd dined at the restaurant and that this amazing thing had happened. The newspaper printed the entire letter, so now the whole city knew about Monday and Tuesday nights. It was like a lottery for my customers. They'd wonder, "Am I here on the lucky night?"

American Express gave us the Promotion of the Year award for our efforts. The place was now swarming on Mondays and Tuesdays, and we would do free dinners just once a month. We did this for about six months before stopping. People still liked the food and our philosophy, so they still went crazy. A lot of other restaurants went on to emulate this tactic.

But the food got the biggest accolades. We won the Silver Spoon award for the best restaurant in the San Antonio area in 1988. And we hired some great chefs. In fact, the guy I brought on as my inaugural chef at Macaroni Grill, Michael Moser, went on to be a high-level executive with Brinker.

One friend of the family, an Italian-American who was about 20 years younger than my father, was going through some hard times. The guy, Vic Paisano, had just gotten a divorce, an electrical contracting company he had owned had fallen on hard times, and he was looking for something that could be a bridge to his retirement. So I said, "I'm opening an Italian restaurant. You can help me." So Vic did the wiring but said, "This place will never work way out here. You gotta be crazy doing this, Phil." (Music to my ears!) After we got the place open, and we were doing well, Vic was still having a hard time. So I told him, "Vic, you know everybody in town. You're an Italian guy and a friend. I'll make you a manager out there." So he agreed.

As it turns out, Vic had worked in the restaurant business with his family a long time ago, and he ended up doing a heck of a job for me. People really liked him, and he played the part very well. He really took ownership—so much so, in fact, that he'd often tell people that he was me! When we started our possibly free meal deals on Mondays and Tuesdays, he'd come up to me and show me all this lipstick on his forehead where ladies had kissed him after he had delivered the good news. Vic is still with the company, by the way.

Aside from the recipes and the texture of my mama Rose's kitchen, another homage to my family was at play at the Grill: My grandfather had always said that Mother Nature makes certain foods taste better during different times of year and that's when we should eat them. We eat heartier in the winter than in the summer. So we established a winter menu and a summer menu, with different wines for different times, too. (Grandpa liked to compare winter wines to the robust, big-busted Sophia Loren and summer wines to the more svelte Audrey Hepburn.) Winter brought more stick-to-your-ribs fare: roasted meats, pork, fowl, and stews with spicier fish and pasta and more robust wines. Come June again, we'd add more chicken and fish with lighter sauces and lots of green vegetables.

We did a promotion around changing the menu twice a year. It inspired creativity by challenging our chefs to come up with unique items.

We continued to do all kinds of crazy things. Once, I hired a high school band to march through. They played one song, "The Star-Spangled Banner," then marched out. Everybody stood up. They were just dumbfounded. It was quite a sight.

Modern casual restaurant concepts have far too few surprises, and Macaroni Grill was going to be the exception. People love surprises. They are tired of the humdrum and ordinary, because they get enough of that. They don't want the same old tastes and the same old flavors. That's why there are so many divorces today. People want things different. They want change. I've heard ad campaigns for certain businesses telling people that they "won't find any surprises here." Is that something to brag about?

Sometimes surprises will just happen if you let them. We had a music student from the University of Texas at San Antonio named Gina working for us as a waitress. One night, on a lark, she sang happy birthday to a customer in operatic fashion. The whole place erupted. She did it again a few nights later. Same response. Bingo! Man, what a perfect complement to our theme, I thought. "Are there any more at UTSA like you?" I asked her.

"Oh yes," she said.

"Well, bring 'em in here, and we'll make them hostesses and waitresses," I said. Operatic happy birthdays would eventually become a staple at Macaroni Grills everywhere.

I make sure I give employees niches that fit their personalities and natural skills and let them excel there and become creative with their specialties. The sum total of individual efforts is what the real "teamwork" in a creative restaurant concept is all about. A restaurant is like football team. In football, every offensive play can be a touchdown if everybody does exactly what they're supposed to do, using their unique talents. The same is true in the restaurant business. Execute and you score every time.

A concept is only as good as its strongest or weakest parts. You can assemble a strong kitchen, a strong floor, a strong front-door presence, a strong office, a strong accounting department, and strong management. But if you've got one weak link, it all falls apart. To hold someone accountable, you must first know if they're capable of being accountable. A common mistake restaurateurs make is assuming that the people they hire already know their jobs. When we are opening a new restaurant, we send people to our own operations classes once or twice a week. We make sure these folks understand profit and loss. We make no assumptions that they'll get it—we test people on their knowledge.

Beyond our personnel, part of the mystique of Macaroni Grill was that you could walk into the place and see plain things like concrete floors and wine in a jug and contrast those with the elegance of flowers on the table, opera music, and fabulous food. We did that so patrons wouldn't be intimidated. By combining such upscale and downscale design elements with all the action, such as our frenzied kitchen, and the sounds, such as the happy drone of the crowd and those operatic waitresses, we created an almost dizzying effect. All the highs and lows created a balance and a few surprises, kind of like at my Italian home.

I had no windows in the Macaroni Grill, as is the case in many of my restaurants. I want to get people away from the outside world. They can't look out and see the world they're escaping from. If it's a lousy day outside, it's still a pretty day inside. I create my own environment and my own world to get them away from all their problems and cares and give them a one-hour or two-hour vacation. That way, I control the mood. If you've ever visited one of the big studio buildings at MGM or Columbia or any of the others around the country, you'll notice that you can't see out. You're oblivious to what's going on in the outside world. Those pros create their own sets and their own moods. So do I. And I don't like to break that mood, even in the bathroom. That's why I had tapes of Italian music and conversation playing in the men's and ladies' rooms at Macaroni Grill and had appropriate language and music playing in my other concepts—Mexican, Asian, etc.

As Romano's Macaroni Grill got going, I used to tell people that I didn't care if I made money on the food, because I was in the wine business. We did about $4 million worth of business a year, and more than 25 percent of that was from wine. (It was around 30 percent our first full year!) My wine cost was about 11 percent, so our $1 million in wine sales cost me less than $150,000. I wouldn't forget this equation at future restaurants.

So much for distributor Alan Dreeben's theory.

When we expanded, we stayed with the jug wine, which was Gallo at the time. People started complaining about the sulfites. So I got on the phone with the Gallo folks and asked, "Will you send someone here to brief me on this and provide me with a brochure or something so I have some information to give my customers?" They never got back to me. So I switched to Delicato, and they gave me a better price and managed our wine program for us. Only then did Gallo get back to me. Years later, I had the opportunity to meet the Gallo family. When I told them about my experience, they were quite embarrassed.

How did Macaroni Grill get to the rest of the country? That's where Norman Brinker enters, or should I say reenters, the picture. I didn't want to build a huge corporation like I did with Fuddruckers. I simply didn't have the stomach to go through all that again. Remember that Norman had dropped by to talk with me at Fuddruckers, but my sister sent him away and I never called him back. Macaroni Grill was just going crazy, so I thought, well, this might be a good time to give him a call. I picked up the phone one day, and when I finally got through to him, I made it a point to say in a matter-of-fact voice, "This is Phil Romano and I'm returning your call." He paused for a moment and said, "Damn it, Phil, that was ten years ago!"

We both laughed. When we calmed down, we had a nice talk. I told him, "I didn't want to call you until I had something unique to share." Then we talked about the red-hot Macaroni Grill. Even though he was leaving on a business trip, he quickly arranged to send some people down to San Antonio, including Lane Cardwell, who was in charge of strategic development for Brinker—then called Chili's Inc.—and Doug Bates, then the company's vice president of food and beverage. We sat down to dinner, and they tried everything on the menu. They loved it.

The group seemed to collectively view the place as the perfect marriage of food, presentation, and atmosphere, and they just went crazy. They said they had better summon Norman as well as another Brinker mover and shaker, Ron McDougal, to Leon Springs right away.

They were intrigued to discover that the average check at Macaroni Grill was $15.50. That was high compared with the $7.00 average at their flagship chain, Chili's.

Norman called from the road and said that Lane was just beside himself about the concept and the numbers I was posting. Norman and Ron quickly flew down to San Antonio. After about 20 minutes, Norman asked, "How much do you want for it? How can we do a deal? Can you come aboard to do this with us?"

Well, I was brash. I had a ponytail. I didn't wear socks. And I was very much my own man. I said, "Norman, I never worked for anyone else in my whole adult life. I'm not gonna do that. I'd come in and ruin your culture." We talked for a while, and he said, "Well, why don't you come in and be a consultant." I finally agreed but warned him, "If you're not going to listen to me, you're wasting my time and yours." We shook hands at that meeting, and in 26 days, we closed the deal.

I must point out that I offered Macaroni Grill to Fuddruckers first, which was only fair, because I was still on their board when I created it. But their executive vice president said they didn't want it. Only then did I contact Norman.

After seeing what happened to Fuddruckers after I sold it, I told Norman that I was still a little apprehensive about this deal, but he assured me that the concept would thrive under Brinker and remain true to its founding principles. I thought I'd stay with Brinker on a month-to-month basis. But that relationship spanned 13 years. I continued to work with them, because they basically left me alone and they let me borrow some of their people when I was ready to flesh out a concept.

I got $5 million in stock in 1989 for selling Macaroni Grill. About a year and a half later, I sold that $5 million in stock for more than $22 million. Remember, I opened that first Macaroni Grill with an investment of $150,000. So I can accurately say I made $23 million on one restaurant!

When I sold it to Brinker, I took care of my people who had made Macaroni Grill so successful and gave them pretty generous allotments of stock in the company. They all did very well with it, including my old pal, Vic Paisano.

The popular "chefs run our company" television marketing campaign, with likeable chefs Aldo and Carlo, was Brinker's idea. While the chefs certainly call the culinary shots at the restaurants, they really don't run the place in the big-picture sense. That's more of a marketing gimmick. However, Macaroni Grill was the first chef-driven operation in the casual restaurant business, and to this day, the chefs have more latitude than at most chains.

Today, the format for all Macaroni Grills is pretty uniform. Patrons still walk down an elevated ramp entry into a bustling scene and get the feeling of instant excitement. There are still displays of fish and cabinets of pasta and other foods. Waiters still write their names on the tablecloths with crayons. And those jugs of wine, just like the ones Grandpa Romano put on our family table, are still there to greet diners. A few irreverent little touches still abound, such as the sign on the backside of the men's room door that reads "W-O-M-E-N."

But the kitchen is in the back, not in the middle or along the sides, to my chagrin. Yes, a kitchen in the middle of a restaurant crowds the place a little, but that's exactly the point. What gives a jet and other high-powered machinery their energy, after all, is forcing power through a small, central space. While the essence of the Macaroni Grill idea remains, other changes have been made to conform with cost savings and convention.

The opera singers are a rare sight these days, and the wine area is gone. They put in booths! If you've been to Italy, they don't eat in booths. The restaurant might as well be a burger place. As the years go by, Macaroni Grill seems to get further and further away from the original. Now, it's starting to look like a Chili's. Some of the flash is gone. I think it needs to get back to where it belongs, with smaller locations in smaller markets. The key to creating a restaurant concept is having great food, followed by location, location, location. After you have enough locations, the key to sustaining it is authenticity, authenticity, authenticity. No doubt, Brinker has changed it over the years. But the company paid me well to forget it. I became content to be a concept creator, or "concepteur," and let other people operate my creations and take them to the moon—or elsewhere.

In 2005, more than 200 Macaroni Grills are operating in 38 states and 5 countries around the world, and Brinker plans to keep expanding the concept. If you ask me, I think it's time for them to stop growing the chain and start concentrating on operating the ones they have. But they still call it Romano's Macaroni Grill, after all. And it's still a great meal.

Another side note: I approached Ron McDougal, who had moved up the food chain to be chairman of Brinker International, when sales were sagging a little in 2004, and said, "Look, my name is on every single Macaroni Grill. I'm still alive. I'm not an ugly guy. Let me lend some authenticity to it and help with the marketing campaign. I'd get up and talk about my family and the kitchen of my childhood." He said, "Well, Phil, we have our own marketing department, and I defer to their judgment." So it didn't happen. It's too bad, because that type of first-person approach makes customers realize a real person brought this thing to life, not just a corporation.

Back in Leon Springs, a place some of my friends would call Philville after I took over all that property and started opening restaurants, I was busy juggling plans in the early 1990s for some of those other quaint buildings.

# 11

# A SETBACK, A REVELATION, AND A CATALYST

**F** o o d   f o r   **T** h o u g h t

No matter what you have and who you think you are,
the most important thing in your life is your health.

**S**ometimes, personal trauma gives you a new perspective on life. That was clearly the case for me about 15 years ago. Death, it seemed, was right around the corner.

It was 1990, and I had just celebrated my 50th birthday. I had forged the successful alliance with Brinker International over Macaroni Grill and future creations I would do for them. Out of nowhere, it seemed, I developed a sharp pain in my side. I was convinced it was appendicitis. My doctor told me that it would just get worse, so he scheduled an appendectomy for me the next weekend. Oddly, the pain seemed to subside—a fact that concerned the doctor more than if it had persisted. He suggested that I come in for a battery of tests.

Well, it was the appendix, all right, but it wasn't appendicitis. A CAT scan revealed a huge cancerous mass about the size of an apple. I asked the doctor to be very direct with me, and

he was. He said, "Go home now and get all your affairs straight-
ened out, because I don't know what we're going to find."

Those words shocked the hell out of me. I had watched cancer take my dad. But I was still relatively young. Goddammit,
this could be it, I thought. My mortality slapped me in the face.
When I was a kid, I thought I was this superbeing. Ha. I was 50
years old, and my time could be up. I had everything going for
me, but I was going to die. I wasn't really scared, however. I was
just mad. Had I accomplished all I set out to accomplish? Hell,
no. Like others who have faced similar diagnoses, I did some serious soul searching. All of a sudden, time held a new urgency.
The days before my exploratory surgery were nerve-racking.

The doctors opened me up. When I came to, they gave me
mixed news. Fortunately, the cancer was pretty encapsulated—
contained. But the biopsy indicated that it was malignant lym-
phoma, or large-cell cancer, though it hadn't actually spread to
my lymph nodes yet. They took out my appendix and six inches
of my intestines. The surgeon said they got it all.

After about a month, I was told I should take chemotherapy
"just for insurance." I went to an oncologist who I'd known for
years, who just happened to be an expert on this type of cancer.
He told me that this cancer was very aggressive, which, while
alarming, was good in the sense that it would attack the chemo
and kill itself in the process. Small-cell cancer is harder to keep
in check and just keeps popping up in other places.

I asked how long all this was going to take. He answered: "Six
months." It was an unpleasant prospect, not just because of the
discomfort it would cause but because I would be on somebody
else's schedule. And I was already angry—angry because I was
supposed to hear about other people having cancer, not have it
myself. I had taken pretty good care of myself. I ate well, didn't
smoke or do drugs, and drank only moderately.

Nevertheless, this was my bitter pill to swallow. Considering
the alternative, I resolved that I was just going to sit down and

do what the doctors told me, which was the first time in my adult life that I'd had to bow to authority.

I went through chemotherapy and had a catheter sticking out of my chest, but I never told my family that I had cancer. I was a vain guy, so when my hair started falling out, I just cut off my ponytail, shaved the rest of my hair off, and resigned myself to looking like a six-foot-high cue ball for six months. The day I did it, I went into work and told my employees and customers that I'd won a wager with a guy who bet me I wouldn't shave my head. I wasn't going to crawl under a rock and hide just because I didn't have any hair.

But I never missed a treatment, even though I hated that feeling of being drugged and listless when the chemicals started coursing through my system. They gave me the most potent doses possible, because they felt I was young and strong enough to withstand it. They said that if I could get past five years, I'd be cured.

When you're getting chemotherapy, there's a peculiar aura about you. You're usually taking steroids along with it, and they sort of puff up your face. You look almost cherubic. People who have been through it noticed those characteristics and approached to quietly reassure me that everything was going to be okay. It's kind of like a fraternity. To this day, I do the same thing with other people in the same situation.

I dodged a bullet, by God. But a lot of things went through my mind when I was sick. I had thought I was going to die, and I began to realize that I still wanted to do much more with my life, and that nothing was more important than your health. I feared that I was going to be one of those "shouldadidit" guys that I was telling others not to be. The experience was like being on a plane that you thought was going to crash. I hadn't been scared, just pissed off that is was going to end this way.

But the anger subsided and was replaced by a new sense of urgency. I had, as they say, an epiphany. I found new impetus and, some say, a new impetuousness. I was resolved to become more prolific in my life. This vow took the shape of a rhyme: "When a thought goes through my head, I better act now, cuz I can't when I'm dead."

I became more of an existentialist. I didn't want the next 50 years to be like my first 50. Yes, I was successful, but I wanted other things. All those little trappings and comforts—that big house on the hill, my cars, the expensive art I collected—weren't as important anymore. The thought of making the most of my time now took precedence.

My bout with cancer had been a life-changing event. I had a renewed passion for life. But for a few years now, I had felt the passion slipping out of my marriage. Libby had stood by me during my illness and was a very good wife, but the conflicted feelings I had about our future together wouldn't go away. I just couldn't suppress the thought that I had to be on my own to move onward and to do some things I wanted to do in the time I had remaining on this earth. Yet Libby had been a big contributor to my success. She had started as a school teacher and became a school principal and is a smart woman. If it wasn't for her, I don't think I would have been able to accomplish the things I did, because she was supportive and always offered a steady income when I struggled to build my restaurant businesses during those early years.

I had a hard time asking for a divorce after 26 years of marriage, but I finally got up the nerve. I felt increasingly as though I was married to my sister. Libby was floored and of course had every right to feel that way. I told her she had been a good wife and hadn't done anything wrong and that I didn't dislike her. Getting divorced was something that just hadn't happened in my Italian heritage, and I didn't think it would ever happen to me. There was a stigma against it, and I certainly would not escape the guilt. Marriage was an obligation. But my desire to exercise my free will and do the things I wanted to do with the rest of my life was stronger.

Libby reluctantly consented to the divorce. I suggested that we call our attorneys and accountants to put two different piles of our assets together and she could choose the one she wanted. She did, and we split everything 50-50. We even had a black-tie party to mark the occasion to let all of our friends know that if a good marriage must end, it should do so on a happy note.

Libby had suffered from endometriosis and couldn't have kids, so we didn't have children to complicate matters. Financially, Libby came out very well. I like to say my actual divorce cost me nothing, but my ex-wife got $50 million from the business deals we split. What's fair is fair. I earned $50 million, too, and started life anew. Libby is still a good friend.

# 12

# MORE GREAT THINGS
# FROM THE SPRINGS

### F o o d   f o r   T h o u g h t

Success not only comes from understanding what will and
won't work, it comes from the understanding of just how broad
a market it will affect.

**I** had recovered from my bout
with cancer, and my creative juices were again flowing freely.
The Leon Springs Macaroni Grill was doing big numbers, and
Brinker was starting to roll out the concept. But I still had several other buildings to play with in my little mad-scientist, test-
town laboratory. The clock was ticking, I had a newfound respect
for time, and I wanted to use my talents judiciously while still
here on earth. So I got busy.

I gave serious thought to opening a fish place in Leon Springs
on the site of a small blue shack in the middle of town. I envisioned a shuck-house there that would specialize in $9.95 live
Maine lobsters, which I'd have flown in fresh daily. Customers
could pay a buck less for a lobster with only one claw, inspiring
the restaurant's working name: Lefty's. But I'd better give this
idea a little more thought, I told myself. Another concept would
feature nothing but chicken: chicken soup, chicken pot pie,

chicken breast, chicken sandwiches, chicken salad, fried chicken, roasted chicken, etc. It would be a country-themed place and would have a giant sign on top with a rooster's head going backward, then forward, in a pecking motion. Appropriately, I'd call it Pecker's. I thought I'd franchise Pecker's with large and small versions of the place: Big Pecker's and Little Pecker's. But I "chickened" out and deep-sixed the shuck-house idea, too. These ideas, while amusing, were too limited in scope. (But that didn't stop a guy, who evidently had attended a speech of mine, from opening a Lefty's on Beltline Road in Dallas about a year later. I had mentioned it as a possible project during my presentation.)

One of the advantages of owning most of a town was that I had the luxury to change my mind about projects with only minimal adverse financial consequences. There were also benefits of clout, in those instances where I really needed to exercise it. When I was in the early stages of putting together Macaroni Grill, I went to a little bank across the street called the Bank of Leon Springs. I sat down with the president and told him that I was doing that restaurant across the street and I thought I'd give him first shot at a working-capital loan of about $50,000 for the project, just to do business with the neighbors and be friendly. He was kind of arrogant and short with me, saying, "I don't do restaurant deals." Okay. So be it. I just went to another bank and had no problem.

During the construction of Macaroni Grill, I went back over to the Bank of Leon Springs and needed to cash a check. He wouldn't do it. "You don't have an account here," he said.

"An account? I tried to do business with you, but you didn't want to do business with me," I said. No matter what I said, he wouldn't budge. "I live in a house up there on the hill," I said, pointing to The Dominion off in the distance. It's one of the biggest houses in San Antonio. I think you can see that I'm good for it." Then I ran down my business track record for him.

"Sorry. I'm not going to cash your check," he said.

So I called one of the owners of the bank, a friend of mine named Stanley Rosenberg, and I told him what happened. "Oh, we'll get on him about that," he said. "Don't worry about it." So I let it ride.

Well, I had previously bought the land of the Rudolph's store in Leon Springs and was now buying the owner out of his lease there. He had a $30,000 line of credit at the Bank of Leon Springs, and I figured we could use that for the place, and I just thought it would be better to leave it at the same bank because all of Rudolph's vendors and suppliers were there, too. So I sent the manager over to continue the deal. The same banker made the manager produce all kinds of financial statements and other paperwork. And after all that, he refused the loan. I went down there to ask him why, and he said, "Because I don't want to do business with you."

I guess he was still pissed off over the check-cashing scene I made. "On what basis? My credit is great," I said. "Oh, on general principles," he replied. "Oh, is that right?" I replied, realizing that my financial statement was probably worth more than the bank's. I left, furious.

So I went back home and looked at a property survey, and a smile crossed my face. I figured out that I had the only water well in the area. I was supplying that very same bank with its water.

So I went back to the place with a business associate who had a partnership account of $500,000 there. I told the banker, "I supply your water, and I'm here to let you know I'm going to cut you off in two weeks. So you've got two weeks to dig another well. And in the meantime, if I see you watering your grass or find out you're using water for anything other than drinking or the bathroom, I'll cut you off immediately. I don't want to do business with you, either." Then the guy who was with me told the bank president, "And I want my money out of here. Now!" The banker started to turn gray. He wasn't so cocky anymore.

Two weeks later, as promised, I turned off his spigot. The next week, I saw water trucks out there drilling a well behind the bank. That thing cost him $45,000. All we were asking for was a $30,000 line of credit. Pretty soon, I got a call from Stanley, the owner, and I told him, "Stanley, I was trying to be a customer of his, I was more than qualified, and he was a complete asshole to me at every turn. He shouldn't be there. He's bad for business." Stanley said he'd take care of it, but I told him, "What's done is done." Later, I helped put a group together to buy the bank. When I looked at my survey again, I realized that the well the banker had dug was on my land!

I continued to take care of business. I had long thought about creating a Mexican restaurant in Leon Springs. But we were in the heavily Hispanic San Antonio area, and there was no shortage of local Tex-Mex restaurants dotting the landscape. In fact, about 53 percent of the population there at the time was Mexican-American. So, I thought, why not open a place that would feel more Mexican than Mexico? The only places you could find authentic Mexican food were some little mom-and-pop places that had virtually no ambience. I thought: We'll speak Spanish to our patrons, serve authentic country-Mexican dishes, and offer some zany twists—a deft combination of authenticity with the Wow Factor.

I had another great name for this one: Nachomama's. And I had the perfect place for it: the old brothel building. We'd serve tortilla chips in hubcaps, make our own tortillas, and offer such authentic dishes as snapper with a sweet-chili crust, rib stew, and Mexican-style lamb shank plus enchiladas and most other mainstream Mexican favorites. Instead of refried beans, entrees would be accompanied by black beans with corn, plus we'd offer a delicious Mexican cinnamon coffee.

It would be a feast for the eyes and the stomach. To give the place a madcap look, we put burlap bags and billboards on the ceilings and strung empty tomato cans as light fixtures. Sandbags would pull the restaurant's front door shut behind entering patrons. Bushels of peppers and other produce rested near the entryway along with bins of onions. Plus rotisserie chickens lined the walls of a visible kitchen. Instead of stainless steel, I used galvanized steel, to give it a more Mexican look. People would come in and see these things, recognize our points of difference, and go "Wow!" The overriding point of difference here was that Nachomama's was not a Tex-Mex restaurant. There were already plenty of those around.

We'd also have a wide assortment of frozen alcoholic concoctions with funny names that we'd draw from colorful frozen-drink machines, using fresh fruit from visible barrels as well. A funny-sounding frozen drink is the one kind of alcoholic beverage you don't mind drinking in front of your family, our research found. Most of the kids working there were either of Mexican descent or were taking Spanish in high school. So I asked them all to bone up on the language and approach the tables speaking Spanish, and if customers didn't understand them, then they could start conversing with them in English. That removed a potential barrier.

We opened in April of 1992 to rave reviews. People loved the food, the irreverent name of the place, and its eccentric culture. The place had a terrific, fun energy about it. There were racy signs hanging over the bar, including "No Farting Allowed," pictures of provocative women hanging in the men's room, plus signs over the urinals that said, "Piss on Drugs." In the women's room, there was a dressed male mannequin. At the end of the night, we'd go into the lady's room, only to find the mannequin's clothes torn off and lipstick kisses planted all over his body!

Brinker execs were keeping a keen eye on Nachomama's and thus far liked what they saw, although I sensed they might want to tone down a few things if they bought it from me.

Meanwhile, my urge to tweak was as strong as my urge to create. Having bought out the Rudolph's gas station in Leon Springs, which was next door to the Leon Springs volunteer fire department, I was trying to figure how to beef up sales there. So we posted signs saying we were going to give a percentage of every gas sale to the fire department. It seemed like everybody in the community came out to get gas (and a few sundries while they were there) to feel as though they were pitching in. We ended up getting enough money out of that to purchase a jaws-of-life tool for them. We also bought a giant popcorn machine, put it in the front window in view of the gas aisles, and offered free popcorn to all our patrons.

Think a little bigger, Phil. What if we put a barbecue pit on the outside of the place and sold barbecue? Texans like their "cue" as much as they do their Mexican food. What the hell. I could attach a barbecue joint to Rudolph's without much problem. But if we wanted to open a barbecue joint, I knew I'd better have some strong points of difference to offer. So I began my research and decided to travel the highways and byways of Texas in a quest for the best way of preparing barbecue.

I drove for days on end. Many parts of Texas, such as New Braunfels, were settled by Germans, and it seems they all had different and unique ways to cook meat. But the best I found was in Lockhart. I had asked the German family owners there if they would like to come to San Antonio and help me open a similar operation, and I'd partner with them. They said they were happy as larks where they were, but they'd be glad to show us how to cook the barbecue. I thanked them profusely, they showed us the process, and we even copied the pit cooker with their permission.

We decided to keep the Rudolph's name, though we did shorten it down to Rudy's, and in August of 1992, our Rudy's Country Store & Bar-B-Q tandem made its debut—one of the earliest cobranded restaurant-convenience store combos.

We offered beef, pork, chicken, sausage, turkey, brisket, chopped beef, and baby-back pork ribs that were fall-apart tender. There was even prime rib. I don't think there was a place in existence where you could buy prime rib for $7.95 a pound like we offered. Instead of the often-used mesquite, we used the slower burning oak wood for a more lightly flavored meat. In the Rudy's cooking system, the fire was built in an outside chamber and the heat and smoke were carried to meat on grills inside. Other cooking processes tend to dry out meat, we felt. Our meat was evenly cooked and juicy. Instead of cooking sauce into it, we treated our meat with a dry rub of seasoning and then slow-smoked it in a wood-stoked pit. We cooked brisket from eight to ten hours and the other meats about three hours.

Because every competitor in the state claimed to have the best barbecue, we cryptically billed ours as "the worst barbecue in Texas." Customers got the joke, and they loved the product. We had a great mix of patrons, ranging from physicians and executive types from nearby Dominion to construction workers, housewives, truckers, and other travelers plus professionals who had driven all the way from downtown San Antonio just to feast on our distinctive product. People could buy the meats by the pound or in smaller sizes. The place was self-service, and all the meats were sliced to order and served atop butcher paper, accompanied by good white bread, chips, fresh onions and tomatoes, and sodas or cold beer. We didn't get into the business of selling all the side dishes like potato salad, beans, and cole slaw like other barbecue places at the time, because our focus was the barbecue itself.

The place was operated by a 40ish African-American gent named "Doc" Holiday. He was an excellent barbecue cook, having honed his skills by preparing meals en masse for hunting groups at a ranch. Although we didn't want to make this a "sauce place," we sampled his personal brand, which was patterned after his mother's recipe, and decided we couldn't afford not to use it. It was a good thing we did. The sauce (we spelled it *sause*) quickly became legendary. In fact, we shipped it by the case all over the world with the following caution on the label: "Don't use before sex!"

We found we'd tripled our gas sales at the station by adding the barbecue—literally beefing up sales, as planned. When we first took over the place, Rudy's was doing about $500,000 annually in total sales. Now, the same place has got to be doing at least $5 million in sales, including the barbecue, and Doc is still as active as ever with it. We took the Rudy's concept to Houston, Dallas, Austin, Albuquerque, and a few other places. We eventually sold it to Creed Ford, the former Brinker COO, and his wife, Lynn. It continues to do well today with numerous locations in Texas and New Mexico.

Not long after Rudy's was catching fire, Brinker decided to buy the Nachomama's concept from me for company stock. They ended up building toned-down versions of it on Park and Preston roads in Dallas and at a location in suburban Plano. But in a bout of political correctness, the name was changed to Cozymel's. Still, we had some fun with the concept. We made up a little archetype folk tale for the place: "Once upon a time, two guys had a grocery store in Cozumel, Mexico," it said. "They sold a lot of groceries. Then they began to make meals, and soon they were in the restaurant business. They moved to the States and wanted to do the same kind of place, but they got the name wrong and now they call it Cozymel's . . ."

Most of the original Nachomama's format was kept intact in the rollout, including the splashes of color. The first Dallas-area Cozymel's had 29 different hues of paint. Its walls and floors were covered with weather-aged planks from an old, second-hand lumberyard. The bar was covered with galvanized tin. New moniker and all, the restaurants started to take off.

I would eventually get $7 million for the Nachomama's/Cozymel's stock from Brinker. But at about the same time they were building Cozymel's, they took a chance on acquiring On the Border, which had become available because it wasn't working out so well on its own. All of a sudden, Brinker had 20 On the Border restaurants and a second, distinctly different Mexican concept, Cozymel's, and they were in a bit of tizzy.

I think Brinker made a mistake in having the same guy, John Miller, in charge of both of them. If a guy has two mistresses, it stands to reason that one is going to get more attention than the other. Hence, he developed On the Border twice as fast. Eventually, Brinker decided to operate Cozymel's as their higher-end Mexican concept and give it a stronger seafood flavor. But in the spring of 2004, Cozymel's was purchased from Brinker by Food, Friends, and Company, which said it planned to expand it.

At about the same time Cozymel's was rolling out, I opened another Italian concept, the family-friendly Spageddies, in Dallas. Actually called Spageddies Italian Italian Food, its price point was a rung above Spaghetti Warehouse and a notch below Olive Garden. The food was cheap and all-Italiano. We baked the bread in-house, and the first loaf was free. You could take a loaf home with you for about 50 cents. Salads and soups were about a quarter each—basically sold at our costs—when they were served with an entrée. We had huge wine casks and would fill up wine bottles to take them over to the table. There were checkered tablecloths and billboards on the ceiling, bocce ball courts, and kids galore. Waiters and waitresses wore fake mustaches and handed them out to the kids. And there were lots and lots of kids.

To my knowledge, we were the first place to "tag" first-time guests, much like churches do when they single out visitors for special treatment. A big yellow flag was placed at the table of new guests. The manager would visit that guest with a personal welcome, and the wait staff was instructed to stand before their table, introduce them to the other diners, and spend extra time with them to help them understand the menu. They would even invite the kids for a game of bocce while the family waited for their food. New customers seemed to appreciate those little touches and the extra effort and made it a point of telling their friends about it, who would come in for the same treatment.

The food was great, and this restaurant was one of my favorite concepts, but there were a couple of problems. Instead of the parents bringing the kids, it became reverse: The kids were bringing in the parents. We were turning into a big babysitter.

Our clientele was families and only families. And we were start-ing to eat the sales of Macaroni Grill. Upgrading would have just made the problem more acute. So I sold Spageddies to Brinker for about $6 million in stock, and they rolled it out. I eventually sold that stock for $10 million.

Brinker took Spageddies to the Pacific Rim and franchised it, then later sold it to Creed and Lynn Ford, who had also bought my Rudy's concept. Spageddies later evolved into Johnny Ca-rino's Italian Kitchen, now owned by Fired Up, Inc. But several Spageddies are still around in Michigan, Indiana, and Ohio, operated by Quality Dining, Inc.

Back in Leon Springs, we opened up yet another business, the Leon Springs Dancehall, in November of 1993. It was a Texas-sized, Western saloon with 18,000 square feet of covered space and a 10,000-square-foot outdoor patio. We had live music, dance lessons, and assorted activities such as volleyball and horseshoes, plus we catered private parties with food from my neighboring restaurants. In fact, it was the only one of my con-cepts born in Leon Springs that wasn't exported, although we did think about it. The dancehall is still successfully operating.

Leon Springs was an unprecedented challenge for me, and a challenge really gets my creativity flowing. My theory that a restaurant in the middle of nowhere would still succeed, as long as it served outstanding food, was indeed borne out. I put these places ten miles outside of town, and people still found them. So I guess it's not just location, location, location after all.

I have also learned that creativity is not only devising solu-tions to problems, it also means improvising and working around handicaps, and certainly, a remote location is a big hurdle to clear. A person who is handicapped figures out ways to use other abilities to compensate. For example, a blind person's senses of taste, smell, and touch become far more acute. If someone can't write or spell well, they think of three or four other ways to express their thoughts besides writing. I like to use another analogy: If you're in a school of fish and you're the slowest fish, you strive to evolve, become an amphibian, get out of the water, and start walking. You adapt.

There's another good example—a modern-day one in fact—about the merits of improvisation. It's about a hypersensitive guy who goes to the dentist for an extraction. The dentist says, "I'll give you some gas, and you won't feel a thing."

The patient says, "Doc, gas doesn't work on me."

The dentist replies, "Okay, then we'll just use novocaine."

The patient says, "Um, no, that makes me break out."

So the dentist says, "Okay, we'll have to give you Demerol."

The patient replies, "Can't take it. It upsets my stomach."

Finally, the dentist produces a pill and says, "Well, then take this. It's Viagra."

The patient looks puzzled and asks, "How is that going to help?"

The dentist answers, "It will give you something to hang onto when I yank out that tooth."

When I got to Leon Springs, I adapted. The town had several old buildings, minimal infrastructure, and little commercial appeal. So I improvised. When I think of my early teachers who stereotyped me as a lazy, daydreaming guy who would never amount to anything and have a hard time adapting, I have to laugh. Though I still had that fear of failure, I was an underachiever in school. But the teachers were the ones who couldn't adapt to me.

It's worse in today's society in many ways. I learned to live around my dysfunctions. I have a short attention span, I could never spell well, and I was probably daydreaming the day they introduced phonics. Today, educators recognize learning problems early and make a bigger issue out of them than they should. They compartmentalize people as "differently abled." All of a sudden, a kid is told he has a problem. He takes it to heart, and it governs the way he approaches life. He begins to believe there are some things he'll just never be able to do. It's part of this competition for victimhood that's been so popular in

American culture in recent years. He doesn't learn to adapt, because society is adapted to him.

By the same token, while I seem to have a lot of creative self-confidence, that doesn't mean I haven't repeatedly questioned my ability to succeed, including in my early days in Leon Springs. That fear of failure never disappears for me, no matter how successful I become. On many occasions, when Macaroni Grill and the other concepts were in development in Leon Springs, I asked myself: "Do I really know what I'm doing here? Or am I just lucky?" Well, I've concluded that luck has an awful lot to do with success. I have been at the right place at the right time on many, many occasions. But part of my "luck" came from hard work and the talents of many who have helped me flesh out my concepts. While I've served in every conceivable role in this business, I remain an idea man at heart. I like to say that I come up with the ideas that others make happen. And the cast of characters implementing them was a big and impressive one in Leon Springs.

I finally sold those "test" acres to Rich Luders, a real estate developer who had partnered with me in my Leon Springs ventures. He was still working the place while I wasn't, so I thought it was fair to sell him my interest.

The same property, which was yielding $400,000 in retail sales when I acquired it, was doing more than $14 million when I left it. All my restaurants are still operating there. If you go to Leon Springs today, it has really grown up and essentially melded with San Antonio. The land has gotten pretty valuable. While I don't own the town anymore, I guess you could say I painted it "red" while I was there.

My Leon Springs mission complete, I moved out of San Antonio to Dallas for a fresh start and to be closer to my work with Brinker International. I also remarried. I met my new wife, Lillie Triche, when she was 21 and managing a Fuddruckers in California. I was 42. Despite my stature and age, she wasn't the least bit intimidated by me, and we became friends. Long after we first met, I found that Lillie had maintained a strong mental image of me just as I had maintained one of her. After my bout with cancer and my divorce, I looked her up again. Seven years after our first meeting, I proposed to Lillie on a trip to New York City as we stood atop the Empire State Building. I gave her a seven-carat ring for each year we had known each other. We were married at The Mansion on Turtle Creek in 1993.

Salud!

# 13

# PUTTING THE *EAT* IN SKANEATELES (A TALE OF TWO ANGELS)

## Food for Thought

People want to feel as though they're privy to something exclusive
and unique, and they like to share that feeling with their friends
and relatives. A little mystique goes a long way in the food-
and-beverage business.

**M**y baby sister, Rosalie, not only helped me out with my restaurant projects, but she worked many years with the Fuddruckers organization. Her last position was as a regional supervisor for them before she finally decided to semiretire to the Auburn, New York, area where we both grew up. I would spend parts of my summers there, and I still keep a house in neighboring Skaneateles that my family enjoys. Rosalie, who was three years younger than me, was a hardworking woman and a tough lady. After a divorce, she raised three kids by herself—with a lot of help from me. She asked me to build her a restaurant in that area that she would run. I was happy to oblige. I wanted a nice place to eat when I was in town, anyway. Besides, when my father was on his deathbed, he asked me to help take care of her.

For Rosalie's restaurant, I found a good location in Skaneateles, a quaint little lakeside village in the Finger Lakes area of New York. The site, on Genesee Street, was a former retail shop that I wanted to convert to an Italian restaurant concept I'd call Rosalie's Cucina, which I sensed the locale populace would love. The building sat next to a little gift store called the Chestnut Cottage, which I thought would benefit from the additional upscale commerce that Rosalie's would generate. But its owner didn't see it that way. I needed to get a zoning variance approved before I could retrofit the place, and he started a campaign opposing the project. I had already bought the building and wanted to start work immediately, so this seemingly needless delay really pissed me off. The guy wrote angry letters to the local paper and appeared before the zoning board, saying my restaurant would attract rats, noise, traffic, and other negatives. I tried to assure both him and the Skaneateles zoning officials that Rosalie's would be nothing but a class act and we would respect everybody's space.

Still, he succeeded in bogging down the case. Meanwhile, I found a better location with clear zoning and no neighborhood issues. But I still owned the Genesee Street building. I said to myself, "I oughta teach this guy a lesson." So I decided to open my own little country gift shop that would compete directly with his gift shop, and I'd put up a sign that said, "Country Store and More. Cheaper than the guy next door."

But I had to get a sign approval from the town board. I went to the meeting at city hall, and the board chairman informed me that the group wasn't going to approve my sign. I said, "But it meets architectural standards. It meets color standards. It meets size standards. My business meets all your other city standards. What don't you like about it?"

The head of board said, "Yes, those things are all fine, Mr. Romano. We just don't like what the sign says." Indignant, I replied, "I thought I saw an American flag out front when I came in here today. I thought this was the United States of America and that we abide by the Constitution. You're abridging my First Amendment rights of free speech." At that point, one of the ladies on the board stood up and chimed in, "The Constitution of America doesn't count in this town, Mr. Romano!" Astonished, I pointed to the city attorney and asked, "Is that on the record?" He said, "No, no, it's not on the record. Go ahead and put up your sign."

So my sign went up, and the controversy was the buzz of the town. Residents got a real kick out of it, but the Chestnut Cottage guy had a fit, I'm sure. Instead of a top-notch restaurant as a neighbor, he now had a hostile competitor that he had helped create. Only in America! I kept my shop open about a year and took a lot of his business away before finally selling the place. As of this writing, a gift shop is still being operated there!

Meanwhile, I had started the Rosalie's Cucina project. Everything was set to go. But then disaster struck. Rosalie had taken ill; soon she was diagnosed with lung cancer. We were all devastated. I asked, "Rosalie, do you still want me to open the restaurant? I can just give you the money, and you can live happily ever after." She said, "No, please build the restaurant, Phil. At least it will give me something to do and keep my mind off things." So I proceeded with Rosalie's Cucina with a heavy heart. But I was all the more determined to make it a thing of beauty, just like my sister.

After extensive travels in Italy, I would build Rosalie's the way I as a patron wanted a restaurant to be. I gave my ideas to a talented young architect named Andy Ramsgard, who had worked on my home in Skaneateles. I'd worked with a lot of architects over the years and saw something in Andy that needed to be cultivated. I asked him why he was working for somebody else. His answer was basically: "Well, because I'm working for somebody else." Andy has a Master's degree in architecture from the University of Buffalo, and he's very bright. I said, "I'll make a deal with you. I'll give you your first solo job and work with you on this project. But there's time pressure. I need you to finish this in four months. I'll give you more money than you would make in a whole year working for this other architect, but you've got to promise me you're going to go into business for yourself." Andy finished on time and did a fantastic job on the Rosalie's design, and he fulfilled his promise to me. Now he's a premier architect and a designer of stylish, high-end custom furnishings that go into his unique buildings. His work has been featured in the *The Stepford Wives* movie remake and in the TV redesign show *Queer Eye for the Straight Guy*. Another talented guy, a Sicilian immigrant, Matteo Bartolotta, made the main dining table at Rosalie's. The place was crafted by artisans.

In our beautiful, salmon-colored Rosalie's Cucina building, we would specialize in serving country-Italian cuisine. The place would seat 120, all in full view of an open kitchen at the back of the place. Rosalie's would feature an intimate downstairs wine cellar, an upstairs Romano Room designed for private parties, a bakery, an outdoor bocce court, a real wood-burning fireplace, and a Mediterranean-style courtyard with a real vineyard and an herb and vegetable garden.

I hired my chef six months in advance, and we put together the menu. Then we arranged for local residents to throw large dinner parties at their homes, with our chef bringing all the food and doing all the cooking. This was a twist on the old preview party idea I had used in earlier concepts. The parties would be attended by as many as the home could accommodate—usually from 10 to 12. We'd show up with wait staff who we had hired in advance, and we'd offer appetizers and pour some of the wines we were going to be serving at Rosalie's. We'd then talk about the restaurant and let people know how it was going to work and what kind of place it would be. We showed them renderings of the restaurant.

We did those parties three or four times a week for a while until, all of a sudden, Rosalie's was going to be their restaurant, and these folks just couldn't wait for Rosalie's to be finished. That recurring theme of ownership had entered the picture again. As Teddy Roosevelt so quaintly said, "I'd rather have people pissing out of my tent than pissing in it." In other words, all of these dinner party people would be part of Rosalie's, instead of outsiders, when we opened. We served over 400 before we even opened the doors.

We opened around Thanksgiving of 1995. Italian music played in the parking lot as patrons walked to the entrance. Our chefs cooked amid hanging ropes of garlic and other bountiful ingredients, while chickens roasted on the visible rotisserie. Our bakery, Crustellini's, produced the pastries and breads we served. Several varieties of sensational goodies were for sale separately at Crustellini's. It wasn't long before Rosalie's was packing in the diners, with the bocce court, wine cellar, and courtyard all serving as holding areas. We served our patrons bread, olives, and cheese to make their waits more tolerable. Rosalie came in most nights to serve as hostess, which helped her momentarily forget her discomfort. The walls at Rosalie's were filled with autographs of customers, including many celebrities, who donated money to the Make a Wish Foundation in Rosalie's name.

A lot of doctors, lawyers, and other professionals living in the area took pride in knowing their wine. So I had them taste my wines and, in effect, create their own wine list at Rosalie's. I had no intention of marking up my wines the standard 300 percent. All I cared about was making $10 for every bottle I sold. Buy a bottle for $80 and sell it for $90. People were enamored by this strategy, which I made sure to publicize. They knew the prices were well under market, and they just went crazy. They'd buy two and three bottles a table because of the bargain. It was like getting a $10 cover per table, I thought. And with the wine prices, they were only too glad to pay market price for the entrees, which were served in huge portions.

Rosalie, who was three years younger than me, died less than a year after we opened the restaurant. The place remains an homage to her. There's a plaque on the wall from me that says, "Built for my sister with love . . . and with way too much money." (About $1.5 million to be exact.) But it was worth every penny.

When I think of Rosalie, I often recall a hotly contested family "sauce-off" we once had. After our family moved from New York to Florida, I'd bring over a group of my fraternity brothers from college on Sundays for my mother's pasta and spaghetti, which she served with her own special sauce that she had worked on all day. These Southern boys just ate it up. One day, we had a sauce contest with Rosalie making her creations and my mother making hers. We would blindfold the testers so they couldn't tell which sauce was which. They tasted them, and we asked them which they liked the best. My sister won. After that, mother never made the sauce again—with a sense of relief, I'm sure. The baton had passed to Rosalie. I think mom was a little tired of doing it, anyway. She was diabetic, and her eyes were starting to go bad. Plus she had done more than her share of cooking over the years. So Rosalie became our Sunday saucier and a damn good one at that.

As part of my vow to my father, I told Rosalie's son, David, that I would put him through Cornell's famous restaurant-management program, only with a few caveats attached. He could make nothing lower than a B, and when he graduated, he couldn't work for me. He maintained his grades and graduated. He became the manager of a steakhouse in a chain. Three years later, he said he wanted to work for me, but I reminded him of our deal. I told him I'd make another deal with him. I was on the board of the Cox School of Business at Southern Methodist University, and I told him that if he passed the test to get into their MBA program, I'd pay for it and supplement his family, because he was now married with a child. He got in, did well, and graduated. But he is not working for me. He is doing well as a consultant.

In 1999, I structured a deal to allow a capable young man by the name of Gary Robinson to buy out Rosalie's Cucina. Gary had been working and managing the restaurant since its inception and had done a great job. In fact, I couldn't have done a better job myself. He has remained true to the concept, and the restaurant does tremendous business and is a great attraction for Skaneateles and all of central New York. We dine there when we're in town, and I still feel Rosalie's presence. I miss her.

However, Skaneateles hadn't seen the last Romano creation. The town had some decent restaurants, but it sure needed a quality hamburger joint, I felt. An old high school football buddy of mine name Johnny Angyal, Hungarian for *angel,* had served as town supervisor but got voted out. He was in his late 50s and confided to me that he was trying to figure out what to do with the rest of his life. I thought about it for a while, and one day I told him, "John, this town needs a good hamburger place. I'll build you one and get it going, and you can buy me out of my position and have a business for the rest of your life." He quickly agreed.

I took over a place on Jordan Street that was previously a Colonial Kitchen restaurant and arranged financing for a restaurant that we'd call Johnny Angel's Heavenly Burgers. The concept would be a lot like Fuddruckers, only smaller, with black-iron grills and folding chairs banked along rows of long tables. Cooked-to-order half-pound burgers and grilled chicken sandwiches would be served on metal trays, sandwiched by fresh-baked buns and topped at an all-you-can-eat condiment bar featuring lettuce, onion, tomatoes, and other toppings displayed green-grocer style. Rolls of paper towels were used in lieu of napkins.

I taught Angyal the ropes pretty quickly and helped him get it up and running. Johnny Angel's opened in 1997. It's a great concept with good food, and it's all Johnny's now. He made enough to buy me out. In fact, he's been mentioned in the *Wall Street Journal* and the *New York Times* and even got on network TV back in 1999. Bill and Hillary Clinton were in Skaneateles for several days, which caused quite a stir, and he put a "Hillary Sandwich" on the menu, which was described as "a little bread and a lot of boloney."

While I can't claim to have put the *eat* in the middle of Skaneateles, at least I raised the bar there.

# 14

# THE FOOD STORE THAT ATE DALLAS AND ATLANTA AND CHICAGO AND . . .

Everybody has the potential to be creative.

**A**s we entered the mid-1990s, one realization about the food industry struck me repeatedly: There was really no place where workaday people could go and get quality food to take home with them. There are some great little delis, but they're limited. There are fast-food places, which gear themselves to take-out but don't offer much in the way of consistently palatable or nourishing food. Throughout the 1990s, I started noticing an increase in the number of patrons wanting their food to go. That meant that they were forced to stand at the bar while we packaged their meals in the kitchen. In most cases, the food wasn't intended to be taken out, which meant that patrons were getting less-than-optimal value and presentation while disrupting our natural workflow and distracting the wait staff.

I've always made it my job to know customer motivation. With jobs and kids and commutes and dual-career families and a multitude of other stresses out there, meal preparation is the last thing on the minds of exhausted people when they get off work. But while people are cooking less, they still desire quality meals. Dining out isn't always the best option for them, because of the strain it puts on their bank balances, time budgets, and their tolerance level for the substandard service that's too prevalent out there. Though food lovers yearn for a restaurant-quality meal, they still want to be home with their families, or they just don't want to make the social commitment to go out. As a kid, it was a treat for me to go out to eat. Now, it's a treat for modern-day consumers to stay home, it seems. Who has time to cook, or for that matter, who knows how to cook any-more? So a growing niche needed to be filled. A problem needed a solution.

What we needed, I started thinking, was a kind of hybrid of the best dining, grocery, and takeout approaches out there. So I pulled together a few industry veterans from Brinker, and we went on an international fact-finding mission. We visited the famous Harrods food hall in London, and the renowned Bal-ducci's and Dean & DeLuca, both in New York. We stopped in some great little out-of-the-way places, too; mom-and-pop bak-eries, stand-alone delis, corner markets, and sandwich shops. Closer to home, we visited Harry's in a Hurry in Atlanta and an ambitious little store in Dallas called Marty's that was basically a gourmet shop and liquor store. Our objective was not to copy them. It was to find out how we could be different. The big ques-tion was: What aren't these businesses doing that we should be doing? We gained a lot of knowledge, and I socked on about ten pounds.

None of these deli/grocery entities really tried to pull it all together. There was no new excitement or unique energy in what they were doing. So back home, I got together with my fel-low travelers and a group of marketing, restaurant, operations, and grocery people, along with a restaurant architect, chef, and a few other experts, to brainstorm about how we could address this new market in a novel way. We had taken pictures, where allowed, in the sundry delis and markets that I explored early on, and pulled together culinary information during what turned out to be a full year of research.

I wanted our creation to have the feel of a great European marketplace, with opera music and concrete floors. I also wanted to make a statement that we were thinking first and foremost about food here, not décor, because food was going to be the décor of this place. I began to realize that this concept was going to be—and would have to be—the boldest creation of my career, a combination of all the experiences and talents and tastes I've encountered, a cross between a deli, kitchen, pantry, take-home-meal restaurant, and upscale grocery store.

During the creation of this hybrid, war was waged between the grocery store people and the restaurant people. Grocery people take care of their shelves and expect the shelves to take care of the customer, we realized. That's like giving your kids a stack of DVDs to watch instead of spending time with them— sort of casting them adrift with no real direction. Restaurants, on the other hand, are more focused on the customer. You often see restaurant managers asking customers how their meals were. You never see the grocery store manager asking how the frozen dinner you bought last week tasted. So the restaurant people won out—sort of. While this wouldn't be a grocery, it wouldn't really be a restaurant.

At a grocery store, people shop with a list. At a restaurant, people shop with a menu. At our new market, people would shop with emotion and impulse. A grocery might have one or two cooks. We'd have dozens of real chefs who would advance a food culture. While it takes an hour or so of tedium to make the rounds at a grocery, we'd make your shopping experience a fun-filled 15 minutes or less. In a grocery store, 95 percent of what you buy has been manufactured someplace else, translating to practically no quality control. With our creation, 80 percent of what you'd see would have been manufactured on premises. At grocery stores, you're cast into an ocean of products, with lines of people buying diapers, paper goods, furnace filters, and other non-food items. By contrast, we would put people in a world of only foods and beverages and maybe some flowers, too, to embellish their dining experience.

At a restaurant, you have to make reservations, get dressed up, sit at the table you're told to, pay a lot of money, and cough up a tip. And in most restaurants (other than mine) customers can't even see the kitchen. At our new place, you'd walk through the kitchen on the way in, and this experience would create value and confidence in the manufacturing process. You have to think twice about what's going into the prepared food you get at a supermarket. Our shop would be a category all its own—a new brand. When people walked in the door, they'd notice several points of difference. The store would be their food universe, their personal chef for a huge variety of ready-to-heat meals they could pick up on their way home, and the next embodiment of America's home-meal replacement arena.

Americans consume close to 30 billion takeout meals a year. In fact, takeout meals actually surpassed restaurant dining in our country in the late 1990s. "Home-meal replacement," which started to take off in the early 1990s, helped bump up those numbers when Boston Chicken, which served rotisserie chicken and home-style vegetables, came along. But Boston Chicken couldn't really be a home-meal replacement operation day in and day out. How many times a week can we eat the same generic chicken? So they became Boston Market and announced that they would broaden their menu and added meat loaf, some sandwiches, and a few other items. But I think they gave the home-meal replacement name a bad rap with operating and food-quality inconsistencies. Plus, none of their food was chef-prepared. Our creation, on the other hand, would be restaurant-meal replacement concept with no limits. People would be able to go out without going out and, in effect, bring home the restaurant.

Also, we'd be offering restaurant-meal replacement, not home-meal replacement. There's a big distinction. The natural foods grocery chain, Whole Foods, has a unique product mix that includes some take-home meals, but do I want to park my car at Whole Foods and navigate past all the nonfood items to get the meals? No. They offer mostly products, not meals.

Brinker and I drew closer and closer to getting this complex joint venture off the ground. We knew we'd have to set a wide variety of price points to appeal to a broad spectrum of demographic groups, from apartment dwellers on a budget to more well-heeled diners. But that didn't mean we'd stock the commonplace. Our concept would be a place where people were familiar with about 80 percent of the food offerings, we decided. The balance would be products they'd find unique. And we'd educate them on these "new" foods to help their palates adjust to new tastes. At restaurants, you can only get what's on the menu. At our creation, there would be up to 1,500 food items. You'd be able to see them and smell them and sample them before you bought them. Hundreds of items would be made fresh daily by culinary specialists. We'd be cheaper than restaurants and more expensive than supermarkets, and that's exactly where we wanted to be. We could become the epicenter for food in any community.

We had our concept outlined. Now we needed a name. Well, the naming of a new eatery at Brinker, by design, is a drawn-out process. The company's creative team and the people who are conceiving the concept will come up with an extensive list of about 100 possible names that they'll splash on an office wall. In this case, four of us were charged with winnowing down that list. During our first naming meeting, we'd each pick 5 names that didn't belong. That whacked out 20. Then we met again. Another 20 got deep-sixed. Yet another meeting: 20 more bit it. We finally whittled it down to three or four. Some of the rejected names, by the way, included Chef á Go Go and Yumbo.

The name we chose, eatZi's, seemed to say a lot and was a near-unanimous pick. (It was my favorite, of course!) Our affinity for *eat* is self-explanatory, but we liked the *Zi's* on the end of the name because it provided a little Italian flair. Because we were both a market and a bakery, we finalized our moniker as eatZi's Market & Bakery. And our slogan following that name, appropriately, would be "Meals for the Taking."

EatZi's started out as a 50-50 ownership split between Brinker and me. As we were building that first eatZi's, Norman Brinker would frequently drive down from his offices on I-635 (the LBJ Freeway) to look at its progress and say things like, "I don't know about this, Phil." I'd reply, "I don't know about this either, Norman. If it works, it's going to go crazy. And if it doesn't work, well, we'll have spent some serious R&D money here." I did know one thing. It was going to look great. There's a saying: "If I'm gonna pull my pants down, at least I want my rear end to look good." And my rear end was going to be in full public view here.

The pilot eatZi's went into a relatively compact 8,500-square-foot building in Dallas, at 3403 Oak Lawn Avenue at Lemmon Avenue, smack in the middle of a busy confluence of culture and cross-traffic. To the west is the upscale Highland Park area, to the east is an affluent gay community, to the south is the downtown area with many above-market apartment buildings, and to the north is more upscale housing.

We opened in January 1996 and hit the ground sprinting, doing twice the volume than we'd originally thought we'd do. Man, were we relieved when it took off! The parking lot was jammed. People came into eatZi's on their way home from work, and when the first thing they saw was all that action and the food, they were energized again. We could literally feel the excitement building, and the press had a field day. People were calling us "the Disneyland of Food" and a "Willy Wonka–like atmosphere for grown-ups." The *Dallas Observer* characterized eatZi's as "a farmer's market, a deli, and bowl-game halftime show all rolled into one . . . ." Another guy wrote, "What the Colonel is to fried chicken, Phil Romano is to eatZi's." One *New York Times* writer even described eatZi's as "the food store that ate Dallas." That's saying a mouthful!

Women were coming up to me at eatZi's and saying, "Phil, I'd like to kiss you. I never have to cook again." Guys were coming up and saying, "Wow, this is great. I won't have to get married . . . again."

Still, it took seven months to get eatZi's into the black. The food costs and the complexity of the operation were imposing. We offered 1,500 fresh products per day in our Dallas location. (Show me a restaurant that has 1,500 fresh products daily.) But we were practically oblivious to start-up expenses. We just cast eatZi's out there. We got it up and running, then worried about costs. That's how I operate sometimes, often to the chagrin of the accountants. But if it's done right, then the people will come and the profits will follow. We projected that the first eatZi's would serve about 1,000 customers a day. It averaged more than twice that the first year. We experienced about $250,000 a week in sales, translating to $12 million annual sales. It was hard for me to leave the place alone. After we first opened, I was in there three or four times a day, tweaking this and moving that, giving pep talks to employees, and trying to create a culture.

In the summer of 1997, we opened our second location at the major intersection of San Felipe and Post Oak in Houston. Both the Houston and Dallas stores cost between $4 million and $5 million each to build, or nearly three times the cost of Brinker's average Chili's restaurant. The expansive kitchen areas, equipment, and vast inventory inflated the costs. Labor costs alone were nearly 25 percent of total expenses, compared with 5 to 7 percent in the typical grocery store. Each store had up to 140 employees, including 20 to 40 chefs and cooks, 10 pastry chefs, 10 bakers, 1 general manager, 3 managers, and 80 or so other support people.

New eatZi's employees go through three different interviews led by three different managers. We challenge our employees to bring new life and excitement to their work. They must try to live their life with personal dignity. And, in the workplace, we want them to practice customer dignity. Treat the customer as they would like to be treated. We also look to see if the employees can take care of themselves and have personal pride. They are empowered to make decisions, so they have to be sharp because we will hold them accountable. We look for very friendly employees.

Despite our high employment start-up costs, our $3,000-plus per-square-foot sales easily outdistanced the $200 per square foot at regular grocery stores. Our profit margins were also hearty. At 12 to 15 percent of sales, margins were more than 4 times the scant 2 or 3 percent that top off most grocery bags. But at around 15 percent, they were several percentage points lower than Brinker's restaurant average, though the typical eatZi's has 5 times the volume of an average Chili's. But eatZi's 3:1 sales-to-cost ratio was outstanding, compared with the U.S. average 1:1 sales-to-cost ratio.

We commonly do in excess of $100,000 on weekend days at the Dallas and Atlanta eatZi's stores. We've had buses full of awestruck French and Japanese tourists visit our locations. In fact, so many curious Japanese were coming in that we put out a couple of tongue-in-cheek signs in their native language that said "No photographs" and "You have to spend money if you're Japanese." A Japanese publisher even did a book on me (in Japanese), mostly focusing on eatZi's. They spent three days with me, going straight down an impressive and methodical list of questions and taking pictures. Several weeks later, they sent me an English-language draft of the book, *The eatZi's Way,* for me to edit, and it consisted mostly of the verbatim interviews. Every time I cleared my throat, they had printed "Huhhuhhuhhum. Huhhuhhuhhum." Talk about detail.

It's little wonder eatZi's is getting so much attention. Walking through the entrance of eatZi's is like entering a quaint, old grocery store. But that's where the similarities end. The first one-third of the restaurant is a full-display manufacturing area, populated by a sea of chefs in traditional white hats, which sort of makes you feel like you're in an Italian movie. The aroma of freshly cooked meals and 20 different, newly baked breads is immediately apparent. The clanging of kettles and the cries of a couple dozen chefs calling out "Hot bread, fresh out of the oven!" or "Soup's on!" adds to the luster. The centrally located Chefs' Case has 50 different platters of food that change throughout the day and a deluxe cold pasta station. EatZi's menus change 25 percent from day to day. A refrigerated case chills a variety of specialty beers from which customers are encouraged to mix-and-match their own six-pack. Sandwiches are elevated to an art form, and most of them are under $5. It was the first time I opened a concept where people were telling me that the food is too cheap. They really wanted me to succeed with eatZi's and were actually willing to pay more for me to continue my operation.

There's a lush produce stand, where our own chefs "shop" to gather ingredients for their culinary creations. People see this and realize that everything the chefs are using is also available to them. Get a made-to-order salad from the Field of Greens salad station, choosing from a dozen different kinds of lettuce. A dozen other separate food stations are jam-packed with visual appeal and seemingly unending assortments of top-of-the-line products. Chefs and their assistants are at your service to help dish out fresh meats, poultry, and vegetables from their pans directly onto the shoppers' take-home plates, plus we have everyday items like meatloaf. There are plastic boats of sushi, bone-in cowboy ribeyes, honey-soy flank satay, poached raspberry salmon, asparagus vinaigrette, and hundreds of other items. It's the Wow Factor multiplied by a thousand!

In fact, more than 8,500 products come through the market per week. There are dishes and variations of dishes you've never seen. Early on, I noticed one eatZi's manager putting Lay's potato chips on the shelves. I asked, "What the hell are you doing?" and he replied, "They're the single best-selling potato chips around."

I said, "But they are too common. We're not going to make this place look like a 7-11. Campbell's soup may also be the biggest seller on the market, but we're not stocking it, either." I told him that the one thing that's going to keep eatZi's unique is discipline. "And one important component of that discipline is to make sure we don't try to put something ordinary in there just to make a little more money," I said.

At eatZi's, we lined off a little "chefs-only" lane that passes by our check stands, and when it's busy, which is frequently, it adds to the feeling of bustle. You're apt to hear, "Excuse me—coming through!" more than once. There are funny, irreverent little signs located throughout the display floor to help keep things light, like, "Betty Crocker just rolled over in her grave . . . this was her wildest dream" and "The only way to get a better piece of chicken is to be a rooster." Sometimes those little added touches help give customers a level of comfort designed to provoke a sense of familiarity and bonding, which in turn stimulates a pleasant emotional response.

We carry a huge assortment of international wines by the checkout area to go with our meals. The food sells the wine. The wine sells the food. It was a huge success component in the concept. Some connoisseurs shop us for wines that they can't find anywhere else in town. In fact, we have averaged about $1 million a year in wine sales alone at the Dallas location.

EatZi's customers are an interesting mix. They range from people who look like they could own the place to people who could rob the place. But there's a commonality. They all like the food. We take care of the person who spends $5 on a meal and the one who doesn't mind dropping $50 on a meal. Sometimes people come in and tell me they met their husband or wife at eatZi's. It's a good people-meeting place. We see women watching for single men who are buying single meals, and vice versa.

One of the tricks we have perfected at eatZi's is cooking our food from 85 percent to 90 percent. If it were fully cooked when we sold it, then it would be overcooked when people microwaved it or heated it in their conventional ovens at home. Although we are selling take-home restaurant meals, there is some outdoor and indoor seating, predominantly for lunch-hour crowds that don't want to eat back at the office. EatZi's is built with both inner and outer "racetrack" loops, so you can either make an easy sweep through the store, if you've come for the convenience of a take-home meal, or make a roundabout path through the food-manufacturing areas for a little more zest and showmanship. At 9:00 PM a red light comes on, and all of the prepared food is sold at half-price for clearance.

For all its complexities, we were having great fun with eatZi's. We opened additional stores in Atlanta, Georgia; Rockville, Maryland; and in the famous Macy's flagship Herald Square department store in Manhattan, plus on Long Island in Westbury, New York. All these sites were highly favored by Lane Cardwell, who had become CEO of eatZi's and who was one of the first Brinker guys to rave about my Romano's Macaroni Grill restaurant back in Leon Springs, Texas. But New York is also where Lane, eatZi's, and I got into a little trouble.

Stores in Dallas, Houston, and Atlanta were all doing well. Lane had told our board he wanted to go to New York City, in the basement of the famous Herald Square Macy's. But, I thought, that's like a young prize fighter winning three fights and now you want to put him up against a champion. The problem with New York is that you can't sell wine in the stores. We were considered a grocery store by state definition, and New York didn't allow alcohol sales in grocery stores. Because food and wine drive sales of one another, we would be compromising the concept. Secondly, we would have limited visibility and be going inside of someone else's core concept with our core concept to make their core concept better. That didn't seem to make much sense.

Brinker's Ron McDougal, who was on the board with me, called me into his office one day and told me, "It looks like we've got to go to New York." I asked, "Why do we have to go to New York?" He replied, "I talked to Lane, and he said he already signed a lease at Macy's." Later, I got with Lane and said, "You know, I don't think this was a good decision. But I'm here to help and to make it be as successful as it can be. But I think if it doesn't work, you're going to be in trouble." We opened in Macy's and at a second New York location on Long Island for additional market penetration.

We opened the Herald Square Macy's to much fanfare, hoopla, and crowds, and it did bring in a large volume of people, but many of the shoppers were eating at the relatively limited number of tables there and not taking the food home. That was a disturbing development, because we wanted them to fill their baskets at eatZi's, not their bellies. It became apparent that the New York stores were going to continue bleeding red ink. We were in the middle of a strong commercial hub, but it wasn't really a heavy residential area. We did a great lunch, but people weren't coming by to take our food home with them at night.

Only after we had put eatZi's in Manhattan did we discover that New Yorkers want to make a beeline home via subway, cab, or bus after work—then shop in their neighborhood. They absolutely would not carry their dinner on the subway or bus, in part for fear of it getting crushed and in part because it might weigh them down if they had a long walk from their drop-off point. We made the mistake of not understanding that.

Our Dallas, Houston, Rockville, and Atlanta eatZi's were averaging $250,000-plus a week, but we could not get the Westbury store on Long Island to top $100,000. We tried management changes and promotions, but no matter what we did, the market wasn't there. People told us that if we'd been about ten miles up the road, it might have been a completely different story. We weren't convenient to the people that could have been visiting us. They just didn't want to fight the traffic. And we couldn't sell wine.

All things considered, we closed Westbury and Manhattan. Some asked why we didn't move to different locations. We thought about it, but without the wine sales, which averaged close to $1 million annually at our other locations, it wasn't worth the risk. Additionally, good locations are hard to find in the New York area. And, once you do find a place to build, there are the unions to contend with that make things about two to three times as expensive. All told, we made a $15 million mistake going into New York. EatZi's obviously was going in the wrong direction.

I'm a firm believer that the team that leads you into a crisis can't lead you out of it. Brinker and I had lost confidence in our management team. In the summer of 1999, we let Lane and eatZi's COO and CFO go. Lane had fallen in love with my concept and was so excited about it that he didn't think it could fail anywhere. He's a smart man who's done terrific work with me, and it was difficult to be upset with him, especially with the way he felt about eatZi's and my other creations. But he took a shot, and if it had worked, he would have been a hero. So Lane left Brinker and went on to serve on corporate boards and enjoy life a little—things people said I should have been doing. We still talk, and I respect Lane very much. But we had a loud wake-up call at eatZi's, and it forced us to put on our britches the right way. I'm just glad it happened early in eatZi's history so we could make the necessary corrections.

My next move was to buy 80 percent of the common stock in eatZi's and take over as CEO. Brinker would no longer be involved in the eatZi's decision making. I had the latitude and responsibility to do what had to be done, and that was to get eatZi's stabilized and profitable and to come up with a new strategy, which I found in creating smaller locations that would feed off of a central locale.

But because eatZi's fell outside of Brinker's casual dining realm, they didn't want to invest in further expansion after that point. So in late 2002, I partnered with an investment group out of Newton, Massachusetts, called Castanea Partners, to buy out eatZi's from Brinker, effectively ending my 13-year association with the Dallas organization. The relationship had been a fruitful one, but being part of a public company—even a good one like Brinker—had gone against my grain, and I was frustrated that I couldn't make the kind of prompt business decisions for eatZi's that a privately owned company could have made. Even though eatZi's was starved for growth capital for a few years, those four eatZi's locations continued to expand their business.

Castanea's comanaging partners, Robert Smith and Brian Knez, the former co-CEOs of publishing leader Harcourt General and the high-end Neiman Marcus Group, showed a lot of faith in eatZi's, and they clearly understood the brand and how to grow it. Another investor, Rick Claes, former Thornton Oil CEO, obviously joined in their enthusiasm. He serves as co-CEO of eatZi's with me. I've become good friends with Robert, Brian, and Rick in the process.

Our group has set out with plans to build satellite locations and some of our larger flagships. In existing markets, we're putting in the smaller stores, which are about 5,500 square feet. Focus group participants had said they don't want to drive from outlying areas all the way into Dallas or Houston or Atlanta on a regular basis to get our products but said they would buy our products if we brought them out to suburbia. So we're doing it. These stores will still contain the standard 3,500 square feet of sales space offered at the larger units because they have much smaller preparation and storage areas, and have the same look and feel of a larger eatZi's. We truck in racks of just-made meals, pastries, breads, and other food all day long from our full-kitchen locations and put it into walk-in coolers. Workers are on hand to plate the product so it can be placed immediately into the chef's cases. This allows us to make food-preparation areas smaller and lower our labor costs. About a quarter of our space at these stores is devoted to wine.

In Chicago's Lincoln Park area, we put up a flagship store much like the one in central Dallas, and we'll branch out from there.

Meanwhile, we're doing over $16 million a year in Dallas and $18 million a year in Atlanta, where we just added a satellite location. We're still running about 2,500 customers a day through those places, averaging $3,000 per square foot in sales with about $16.50 per transaction and an average of four to five items per basket. The other stores are building sales and profitable. We've also added catering services.

In retrospect, eatZi's may have also been a little ahead of its time, like other things I've created. Fifteen years ago, would home-meal replacement or restaurant-meal replacement really have worked? Probably not. EatZi's is just now coming into its own, and the sky is the limit for national expansion. We have just scratched the surface. Home-meal replacement is over a $75 billion business that's expected to more than double in size before the end of this decade, making it the fastest growing segment in the food service industry. Today, we're in the right place at the right time.

In 2005, we plan to add about 30 new units over the next 5 years, averaging $1.5 million each to build, instead of the weighty $4 million to $5 million that the flagship stores cost.

People keep asking me if I would like to own 100 percent of my market in the home-meal/restaurant-meal replacement segment. No, I wouldn't. If I open a hundred eatZi's doing the business we're doing, I would have a $1 billion market. But I'd much rather get other people into this category with me. When they start opening up stores, all of a sudden it becomes a $20 billion category. All I want is half of that market and to be its leader. It almost sounds like a plot. In fact, it is. Who is stealing the great chefs of America? That's easy: eatZi's.

*C h a p t e r*

# 15

# FAILURES AND DISAPPOINTMENTS (PART II)

---

### **F** *o o d* *f o r* **T** *h o u g h t*

Despite your best efforts, things can go askew on any given day or
night in the restaurant biz. When I hire managers, I often give them
a verbal test. One of my questions is: "It's a busy Saturday night, and
the restaurant is jam-packed. All of a sudden, the assistant manager
gets his finger caught in the potato slicer. What do you do?" Their
answers: "Put a tourniquet on it," "Take him to the hospital," "Send
him home," and, "Have him lie down in the office." But I always
shake my head and say, "No. No. No. Wrong answer. You fire the
both of them. That's fraternization on the job!" The look on their
faces when they realize they've been had: priceless.

**F**ood service is a high-risk invest-
ment, and that's no joke. But the people who spout off those figures about 90 percent of all restaurants failing in their first year
are simply wrong. That misinformation only makes it tougher
for some talented entrepreneurs to get loans. The truth is, the
failure rate is no more than 30 percent that first year, probably
a little less. Most of those eating businesses that fail are simply
undercapitalized. Sometimes, there's no righting the ship.

Sometimes, the people involved with you spiral out of control. Sometimes, your business just wasn't meant to be. Here are a few more ideas that didn't quite work out.

## WILD ABOUT HARRY'S

When we lived in the Highland Park area of Dallas, Lillie and Sam used to come home just raving about this little custard place on Knox Street where they stopped almost daily. Sam in particular just loved it. I had to see for myself what the fuss was all about, so I stopped in at Wild About Harry's one day. The owner, Harry Coley, makes an exceptional frozen custard using his mother's recipe and serves giant, old-fashioned hot dogs made of beef brisket, smothered with anything you want. I stopped in several times, enjoyed the taste and uniqueness of the product, and realized that Harry had a nice thing going. He was 60-ish and bubbly, like a latter-day Orville Redenbacher, and he was very customer oriented. One reviewer described his operation as "one of the few places in town where Pleasantville is real." A lot of people said that Harry's was reminiscent of their favorite ice cream parlor where their mother and father took them when they were kids.

I finally met Harry formally, and he told me he'd wanted to broaden the sales of his trademark custard product and expand his concept but didn't know how, and he said he could use my help. I said, "Harry, I don't want to do too much of anything unless I'm sure I'll have a fun concept going, have a good relationship with the people involved, and feel comfortable with them." We talked some more and had dinner a few times, and I really came to like what I saw of him and his operation. So I agreed to go into business with Harry.

We had some fun ideas for the new stores. We'd put the custard machine behind glass and have an employee in a white coat and hat making the custard in full view of patrons as part of our fun presentation. Hence, customers would recognize that Harry's product is freshly made on the premises, unlike at many ice cream places. All the employees would wear nametags that said "Harry." The young woman behind the counter taking your order would be named "Harry," even if her name was Heather, and the 25-year-old guy named Hank who was running the place would also be a "Harry." There'd be pictures of famous Harrys in history: Harry Truman, Harry Houdini, Harry Connick, etc.—even a donkey (Harry Ass). We'd handpick MBA grads and students from the Cox School of Business at Southern Methodist University in Dallas, where I am active on the board, to run the stores. That would help with continuity and give us some smart managers who could become executives.

Wild About Harry's was setting itself up as a perfect mom-and-pop-style operation for franchises and for product distribution. If we packaged the operation properly with Harry's image, built a quaint little icon for the operation, got some solid public relations and word-of-mouth behind it, and got the custard in some stores (we put it in eatZi's), then we'd establish a distinct brand, and there'd be no stopping us. The next step would be to make it a national brand.

We got a couple of Wild About Harry's stores up and running in 2000 in the Dallas suburban cities of Richardson and Plano. We planned to move the company forward quickly. The stores would be about 1,600 to 1,700 square feet in size, centrally located in strip shopping centers, and they wouldn't be particularly expensive to open, we felt.

Just as we were taking steps to mass-produce the custard for nationwide sales, I got a disturbing call from the Dallas Schepp's Dairy while I was away in Florida. Schepp's, which was going to manufacture the custard for retail distribution, was in the process of working through the formula to produce viable samples. But the Schepp's representative told me the recipe that Harry gave him was missing ingredients necessary to produce custard. "This isn't going to work," he said.

So I quickly called Harry and asked if had given Schepp's the recipe as agreed, and he said, "Yah, I gave them the recipe." So I said, "Did you give them the right recipe?" He said, "Well, Phil, we gotta talk about that." I guess he got cold feet and couldn't bring himself to part with his family recipe. Well, I was furious because I had been deceived. At this stage of the game, it was too late to turn back. I had invested $1.4 million in this venture. I was disappointed in Harry, to say the least.

I figured he had until the time I got back in town to get the right recipe to Schepp's, but he failed to do so. We arranged to get our lawyers together to sever our business relationship, and we entered arbitration, where Harry admitted that he had violated our agreement. We had him dead to rights, and I could have put him out of business, but life is too short to hurt people that way. Besides, Harry is a local hero, and I didn't want to be the bad guy that shut him down. Although the two Harry's locations we opened have closed, his original business remains open, and I hope he does well with it, especially because he has to send me a check once month for ten years to help me recoup my loss. Whenever he signs one, I do want him to be reminded of what he did. It's too bad it had to end that way.

## WÉ/OUI, OUI/WÉ

Another idea that came to me in 1999 arose from a solution to a repeat problem I'd encountered in French restaurants over the years. The portions were tiny, the checks were high, the service was snooty, and the atmosphere was formal and pretentious. So I decided I was going to give people a French restaurant that was the exact opposite. It would have big portions, modest checks, gracious service, and a casual, fun atmosphere. First, I traveled extensively in France to observe and prepare.

Thus, Wé/Oui, Oui/Wé, accompanied by the tag line "French Food Everyday" was conceived. (The accents went over the Wé just for a fun twist.) And I even found a French-looking building, The Crescent Hotel, at the corner of Maple and Mc-Kinney Avenues in Dallas. The hotel needed a good replacement restaurant tenant, because Sam's Café had moved out.

We'd have an art deco motif, I decided. And we'd have lots of reds, blacks, and whites; a giant wine rack that climbed a wall next to the long, open kitchen; clocks that told time in cities from Paris to Honolulu to Calcutta to Bombay; and our ruby-red "lips" logo showing up here and there. The waiters would be extremely friendly and speak with French accents, some of them faux, some authentic. Our "show" would be a fun one. The typical American meeting a typical French person may not have a very good time because of the language barrier, I concluded. But if you go to a restaurant and the waiters and staff speak English with a French accent, it's kind of sexy, not to mention much easier to communicate.

We had a long marble bar not far from the hotel elevators that would attract guests for late-night and after-dinner drinks. In the restrooms, we'd have recordings of "common" English phrases that were first said in French, like, "Will you meet me here tomorrow night?" or "Have you tried the roast duck?" and, somewhat cryptically, the old, "Do you come here often?" I even got a fun little dig in: "Italians are better lovers than Frenchmen."

People wouldn't have to dress up to dine at Wé/Oui. There would be no intimidation factor—no attitude problems from the servers. And patrons wouldn't need a magnifying glass to read the menu or see the food. All of our $15 entrées were grouped together, our $18 items were grouped together, and our "market price" items were grouped together—all to help make things even more simple and straightforward. Truffles, mussels, capers, and pate de foie gras would find their way into an assortment of dishes. There would, of course, be frog legs, crépes, escargots, pommes frites, plus some Ameri-French dishes, all served in overly generous portions. A miniature caramel Eiffel Tower would loom over some desserts. Baguettes and a broad variety of cheeses and wines were readily available. No one left hungry.

We opened in late spring of 2000 to upbeat crowds and a young clientele in our bar. We were a lifestyle concept, and one distinctive promotion caused quite a stir. Late at night, we'd pass out little packets that looked like matches, containing our lips logo. The back cover said, "From Wé/Oui for your Wee Wee." Inside was a kiss-of-mint condom and a note that said, "We support the effort to eliminate the spread of sexually trans-mitted diseases. We value you as a customer . . ." This was a lit-tle racy, perhaps, and a few folks didn't cotton to it. Others had a good laugh and pocketed a bunch of them.

I thought, well, we don't have a cigarette machine in the place. And when you come to think of it, condoms save lives and cigarettes kill.

Sacre bleu! Wé/Oui didn't work out, despite the many points of difference. The place looked great, but the location—and perhaps the timing—were wrong. And it didn't help that the road in front of the hotel was under construction for what seemed like an eternity. But I won't make excuses. I wasn't afraid to button it up. In fact, we had a big closing party, and I invited my loyal customers. We had about 400 in attendance, and they all helped me celebrate losing $2.5 million. We ate through our remaining inventory, finished the booze, and kissed the red lips goodbye, and I just chalked it all up to an R&D adventure that didn't have a happy ending, despite those condoms. But life is just too short to continue kicking a dead French horse. Now closed: Wé/Oui. And we have two reasons for not liking the French.

## LOBSTER RANCH

I had been tossing around the idea for another casual sea-food house for years but only started thinking seriously about it in the late 1990s. I still had fond memories of the Old Shuckers restaurant I opened in Palm Beach in the mid-1970s, a place I initially wanted to call Mother Shuckers. Busy with other projects, it wouldn't be until 2001 that I started putting together a plan for Lobster Ranch, which would feature a "buckin' lobster" as a logo. A developer called me and said he owned a center on Preston Road in North Dallas that he wanted to do something with, and I thought this would be a good opportunity to try out the seafood concept. So he and I went in as 50-50 partners. We scored a coupe by latching on to noted local chef Tom Fleming, who had been known for his culinary expertise at a pair of local haunts, The Riviera and Lombardi Mare.

Lobster Ranch was cast as a New England-style seafood house, although we'd offer chicken, grilled Italian sausage, pasta, and other items for nonseafarers. Entrées would range from $5.95 to $25 and feature live Maine lobster, steamed or grilled. You could get a one-pound lobster with new potatoes, steamed broccoli, and corn on the cob for only $18. We'd offer bibs to diners to counter the inevitable butter splatters. We'd have lobster roll sandwiches and plenty of other seafood favorites. Our widely varied menu would feature fresh catch of the day choices ranging from salmon to trout to grouper—whatever was freshest that particular day.

On the design side, we set out little kitschy touches about the place, such as wooden shutters on the walls and a wood stairwell with "timbers" for rails, suspending a giant tropical fish sculpture. At the top of the stairs was a raw bar with shrimp and shellfish on ice and a serving bar area decorated with wooden panels featuring liquor and wine crates. We also had the requisite visible giant lobsters in the tank.

We opened in March 2002. Our points of difference were many, but we had our problems, too. Lobster Ranch was caught in that nether area between a "down-and-dirty" and "fancy" restaurant, and we struggled to find our niche. Some of our customers complained that they found our location inconvenient.

And my not-so-silent partner came in and regularly issued orders to employees and managers, which I felt disrupted operations more than helped. I asked him to stop, but he persisted.

All things considered, we shut the place down in August, just six months after opening. Toward the end, a lot of disappointed customers came by to say Lobster Ranch was their favorite seafood place. Still, we were losing an ocean of money, so I told them, "I sure like you guys, but I'm not going to pay you to come and eat." So Lobster Ranch went into the tank and our "buckin' lobster" was cast back out to sea. But it had pinched me hard for $600,000.

I've had my share of failures, most of which have been outlined in these pages. But something inside me has always said to get up, dust off, and move on to the next challenge with a positive attitude. Life is far too short to dwell on the bad calls you've made. Negative thinking can kill you, and it can infect others. I see it happen at restaurants and other operations all the time. I advise people in the business to dream big, imagine their success, and imagine the success of the employees around them. Negative thinking is toxic. But enough with failures. There are more successes to come.

# 16

# A STEAKHOUSE FOR SAM

**F** *o o d* *f o r* **T** *h o u g h t*

I strive to give customers a level of comfort designed to provoke
a sense of familiarity and bonding, which in turn stimulates
a pleasant emotional response and a sense that they're at home
in my restaurant.

If there was a textbook way to open a Romano restaurant, I followed it in the creation of Nick & Sam's steak and seafood house in the former Lawry's for Ribs restaurant building, just north of downtown Dallas on Maple Avenue. We realized that Dallas had a lot of expensive steakhouses with very good food, but they seemed to be such gloomy places. Were these long faces necessary? Must eating a steak be such a solemn occasion? No and no. So we set out to make Nick & Sam's more festive.

My partner in this venture, a young man, had come to me and said he'd like to operate a restaurant company. I said, "That's good, because I want to keep on creating concepts, and I need someone to operate these things." He said, "Fine, that's what I want to do." So we launched Nick & Sam's with me as the concept creator and patriarch of the place and this young man as operator. I gave him a 10 percent interest in the place.

My partner and his wife had just had a baby son, Nick. My son, Sam, was still a tot at the time. So the place came to life as a reverse legacy of sorts to our kids: Nick & Sam's. Originally, it was going to be called Samuel's, but we thought that sounded a little uppity. We also considered Sam & Nick's, but it sounded like an exterminator's. Nick & Sam's sounded better.

While the restaurant was in its development stages, I took young Sam out to New York to visit his grandmother, whose health had been deteriorating slowly over the past few years. He was just two years old then and probably doesn't remember much of that period. When Mom really took ill, doctors called me three different times, basically saying she was on her last legs. I rushed out there each time, and each time, she got better. One of the doctors said it was amazing that she kept pulling through. My aunt had been trying to comfort her, telling her everything was going to be all right because she'd soon be with Samuel, my father. "Maybe that's what's delayed her," I said, jokingly of course.

The fourth time I got the call, I sensed this was it. I got there, out of breath, and 20 minutes later, she passed away. She had waited for me. Mom lived to 83. She was a good woman, a good mother and wife, and a great guiding force in my life. The hospital where she died in New York was the same one where I was born. It reminded me of how much her life and my own were linked. We'd come full circle. And she got a chance to know Lillie and to see Sam, who was born in 1996—a latent grandchild if there ever was one.

When I was small, I remember how my sister Rosalie and I would go to church with my mother, but my father didn't go very often, though he would sure get mad if we kids didn't go. One Sunday morning when Sam was about four, he was reluctant to get dressed and said, "Dad, I don't want to go."

I asked him, "Don't you want to see God, Sam?"

He shot back, "No."

So I asked him, "Well, why not? He's good, he's nice, he loves you, and he loves all of us."

Sam said, "I go to see him. But he never comes out!"

I laughed, realizing his response was probably genetic. I'm sure I blurted out the same kind of thing to my mom when I was his age.

One of the recurring subjects that Sam and I talk about on our way to his school every morning is how to treat people. I tell him he should try always to say something nice to people. "Tell them something good about themselves. That way, people will like to be around you. It also helps you find the good things in people." When he was a little older, I encouraged him to try also to tell people something that would put a smile on their faces, like the jokes I like to tell. He looked at me and said, "Daddy, your jokes suck. People only laugh at them because you're the boss. If they didn't laugh, you'd fire 'em."

Ouch!

Soon, I turned my attentions back to my son's namesake restaurant. To get Nick & Sam's ramped up, we handpicked our entire team, from the chef to the general manager and the wine steward, bartender, and wait staff. For example, if we liked how we were treated at lunch or dinner by a restaurant worker somewhere, we'd ask for a business card or give them one of ours. That way, we knew from experience and reputation what these people were capable of doing. We hired our headwaiters the same way, then let them put their teams together in that fashion. When restaurant people heard about the concept, we had hoped they'd beat a path to our door. Many did. As a rule, I like to hire people who have already experienced some of the highs and lows of the business or people who have been in business for themselves and had to tough it out—workers who have not had that safety net under them all their lives and who respect the challenge of creating or nurturing a concept to success. Using such an approach, we landed some dedicated people at Nick & Sam's who really knew how to take care of the customer. We made it clear that the entire team was essential to the restaurant's well being, but only through their outstanding individual personal efforts would we succeed.

I don't want employees to work for me; I want them to work with me. Teamwork is a fine and noble concept, but I still have to get my employees to think like individuals. In a team, I have five people who think their objectives are all to think the same. I don't need them thinking the same. I need them to think differently. Teamwork can inhibit creativity, because the team will restrict what you do. It keeps you from going out of the box. When I get a staff together, I don't want them to be like me. If you want everybody to be just like you, then they will limit themselves to thinking just like you. I just want to be the guy who says yes and no to their ideas. I want people to be able to lead themselves and come up with their own ideas.

From the start at Nick & Sam's, individuality was our forté. We set out to establish a wide-ranging wine "cellar" that would feature more than 300 different wines. It greeted patrons as they walked in the lobby-bar area near the front entrance and helped occupy those awaiting a table, plus it provided the perfect, relaxing after-dinner setting. We were trying to put the romance back into wine. People could read about the wines they were curious about on computers along the wine area's side wall. There were wine facts, how many bottles were produced, and other data. Patrons could sample the wines that they wanted with dinner. We offered free caviar in the bar. Some of my business cronies were telling me that it was crazy to give away something this costly. Hearing that, I knew I was on the right track. Free caviar equals *we get talked about.*

We know which wines go with steak or swordfish and which ones complement which sauces, and we wanted to share that information with our patrons up front. Wines, after all, are fermented grapes, and grapes are food. So when we serve wine with dinner, we are putting food with food. At Nick & Sam's, we made sure that these foods do not assault our patrons' taste buds. We even had a price-negotiable policy on every bottle over $400, because I thought people would have fun with that idea. The wine stewards and managers knew what we paid for each bottle, so they could sanction a little lower price. Or patrons could just sip the gratis port we'll set on their tables, if they like.

A baby grand piano, serving as a highly functional conversation piece, sat right in the middle of our open kitchen, in full view of diners. We thought it would be a fun dichotomy for patrons to hear an accomplished pianist playing soft melodies and classical numbers while watching the chefs on both sides of the piano dole out dishes to our waiters, who in turn have to jog to the side of the piano to get past, deftly juggling food orders. New waiters had to acclimate themselves quickly, or else!

Nick & Sam's had a long main dining room, arched ceiling, U-shaped kitchen, and large rounded lights on the ceilings. It was an interactive restaurant with booths facing out toward the dining floor. Décor was tasteful and upscale but far from stuffy. Earth tones, colorful art, and black-and-white prints added some zest. While other restaurant people tear out their hair over such issues as human resources, real estate, payroll, and zoning, my mind tends to drift to more abstract areas like imagery, energy, color combinations, spatial relationships, and even the realization of dreams. These environmental elements bring more joy to the dining atmosphere and help spur lively conversation. People welcome this at Nick & Sam's because they are tired of the same old solemn steakhouse themes. I have a saying: If you want a nice quiet dinner, go to a funeral home!

There was also a 12-seat raw bar adjacent to the kitchen and another, smaller room right off the kitchen called the Chef's Room, which can seat a party of 12. It's called the Chef's Room because it is dedicated to the great chefs of Dallas and features framed glossy photographs of many of them on the walls.

The stage was set for Nick & Sam's. Now it was time for the show. When we opened in the spring of 1999, we decided not to advertise and just let Nick & Sam's go on its own momentum. That way, we could keep up with the place and concentrate on food and service. We would open only for dinner to maintain a clear focus. I was in no hurry to become successful there because I already am successful. Nonetheless, it was an instant hit.

All told, Nick & Sam's cost about $3.4 million to get up and running. But I got most of my cash outlay for Nick & Sam's from the Republican agenda in late 1999, with its capital gains tax changes and other tax considerations. I was able to use the money I saved on a $14 million capital gain—equivalent to about an 8 percent tax break—to open Nick & Sam's. If I'd paid Uncle Sam that money, it no doubt would have been spent on one of the government's many giveaway deals, and there would have been little or no economic ripple. Now I'm paying sales taxes, liquor taxes, employee taxes, and the income taxes on the restaurant's profit. I can give people jobs and train them—I employ about 85 there—and advance people in their careers. Plus, I'm paying thousands of dollars to food and beverage suppliers. And those people, of course, are turning some of that money around and investing it in their businesses. All this economic activity helped stimulate the economy.

It's not unusual for us to do 500 dinners a night there now. It's been a real treat to see people enjoy it and hear the *wow* word thrown around so liberally. Its popularity is a little scary. You don't want to try to juggle too much business and chase the regular customers away, but I think people like to be a part of the crowd in a good restaurant. They like that excitement—they like being part of the special group that is privy to a good thing.

Earlier in my career, I had a kid come to me who had worked at one of my restaurants a while and said he was ready to move up to manager. I said, "Okay, but first I'm going to give

you some money, and I'd like you to go off to four or five restaurants. Have dinner and drinks and just observe what makes
these places so successful. Then I want you to come back and
tell me what you found."

So he came back about a week later, and I asked him what
common denominator they all shared. And the young man
said, "Well, all of the ones I went to that were successful were
also very noisy. But it was the people that made the noise." I
thought about it a second. Boy, that was the right answer, even
though I hadn't really been able to verbalize it until then. It's
that din, that clamor, that excitement and energy of cheerful
conversation, plus the bustling clatter of plates, that seems to
give a restaurant long life and make it successful.

T. Scott Gross, the customer service and salesmanship guru,
said in his book *Positively Outrageous Service,* published by Dearborn Trade Publishing, that when a person visits one of my operations, "You'll see employees who are actually having fun.
There will be hugging. Sometimes lots of it. But the food will
be delicious, and the surroundings will be neat. Because the fun-
damentals demand accommodating the customer, [my] twist is
that the customer should be accommodated in a way that has
never been done before." Amen.

Nick & Sam's was doubly exciting to me, because I was able
to give some enjoyment to the people in my community. The
reviews of the place came out and were highly favorable—as little stock as I put in them. But we did get great reviews from
every publication that visited us, and the place is always crowded,
even on those traditionally slow Monday and Tuesday nights. In
fact, Nick & Sam's had been open less than six months when
the highly regarded *D* magazine placed us among the top restaurants in the city. The magazine also named us the top new
restaurant in the city in 1999.

At the end of our first year in business, we celebrated by giving out about $50,000 in free meals to our good customers. We
gave a card to about four or five tables a night that thanked

people for being loyal customers and making Nick & Sam's successful, telling them we wanted to pick up their check. That got some great reactions. So did our negotiable-price policy on wines. A guy came in and ordered a $1,800 bottle of wine. He said it was great and wanted to look at the wine menu again. He found a rare vintage priced at $2,600. "That's a nice bottle of wine there," he said. Our manager said, "You want it? $2,200." He said, "I'll take it." What did we pay for that? Nine hundred dollars. We were more than happy with our margin, and the customer had a good time. Negotiation also puts a little more fun and romance into the wines.

However, my operator changed his mind about our operating agreement. He just wanted to create restaurants. "This is not a good relationship because we both want to do the same thing, and I think I'm better at creating restaurants than you," I said. So we dissolved our partner relationship and went our separate ways. I still call the place Nick & Sam's. It's a good name, and we're going to keep it.

I brought in veteran restaurant general manager Joseph Palladino to be my managing partner. His 13 years of experience in the business, including a stint at the MGM Grand Hotel & Casino in Las Vegas, have proven invaluable, and Joe really understands the "show" element of this business. Joe helps keep the place exciting and comes up with new products all the time, like the bone-in filet and the dry-aged, 24-ounce, long-bone rib-eye, a cut he discovered in Chicago. He also is a good people person and can make everyone feel like it is their restaurant. Samir Dhurandhar, a graduate of the acclaimed Culinary Institute of America and former executive chef with Sfuzzi in Dallas, is our chef.

I own only 70 percent of the business; Joe owns 25 percent and the rest of the staff owns 5 percent. Ownership gives their efforts an added oomph, which translates to better service for the customer. You've got to find a way to give them a piece of the rock—make them part owners. You've also got to go out repeatedly and tell them how good they're doing. Pat them on the back. If you think they don't care about such things, think again. Don't just do it the first few months you're open. If you don't make employees feel wanted, there's a business down the block that will gladly take them off your hands.

Before I could really cut Joe loose and give him the run of the place, I had to gain confidence in him. So every morning for the first six months we were there together, we'd take long walks in the morning for an hour or so. During that time, we'd talk about the operation and the way I thought. We'd talk about philosophy, business, work habits, and morals. I got to trust Joe and felt he could run other restaurants that I create.

The numbers have always looked good at Nick & Sam's. We finished our first year with over $4.5 million in sales. In 2004, we did well over $7 million, and in 2005, I think we'll do close to $8 million. We are quickly becoming an institution in the city and have become known as a place that takes care of its customers. In fact, the day after 9/11, we handed out a letter to our patrons telling them that we were proud of them for coming out and doing their part to keep the economy afloat. We told them the meal was on us and thanked them for their patriotism. One table was full of people from New York who had been stranded there. Some of them cried. We also did a benefit dinner for the widows of cops who died in 9/11. We raised $25,000.

Our upscale patrons at Nick & Sam's are used to being pampered just about everywhere they go. And while I must live up to my reputation with this group and ensure that they have an enjoyable time, there's also a subsegment of folks who come here for an evening of gracious living that's a wee bit beyond their means. They come for special occasions, expecting that our food, atmosphere, and service will be extraordinary. Part of our responsibility is making sure we live up to, and even exceed, the expectations of these diners. For people who have scrimped and saved to spend their special night with us, I would be acutely embarrassed if they didn't have a great time. I have the responsibility to make sure they always get their money's worth and that Nick & Sam's is something they will always remember.

I have constantly tried to get better and better at everything I do, and Nick & Sam's is no exception. Improvement is a continuing process that is never complete at any of my restaurants. Two things can happen when you try to get better. One, you're going to get better, or two, you're going to stay the same. Conversely, two things can happen if you don't try to get better. One, you're going to stay the same, or two, you're going to get worse. While it's clear to me which option is the most palatable in the restaurant industry, it continues to amaze me how many restaurants and chains put out millions of dollars to get a good thing going but fail to look after it. Then they close and say they don't know what went wrong.

The longer I've been in the business, the more I realize that it's much easier to become successful than to stay successful. Success can make people cocky, inflate their ego, and illuminate their vanity. You can begin to feel that you're infallible and even start taking the customer for granted. I started to fall into some of these traps at different points in my career but always manage to snap back to reality. Running a restaurant is like being a good parent—you're always on the job, keeping up with your creation. If you stop, trouble follows.

Nick & Sam's will always have a special place in my heart. This is one restaurant I'm going to keep and eventually hand off to Sam. If Sam works there when he gets older, he'll be expected to work three times as hard as anybody else. I'm committed to instilling in him the will to succeed. That's a tough thing to teach. It doesn't come by birthright. One day, when Sam was about four, I asked him what he will say when he's older and owns the place. "Welcome to my restaurant," he exclaimed. "I hope you enjoy the food."

When he got a little older, I told him we were going to the kitchen to help wash dishes to practice up for later. He said,

"Dad, I'm not going to work back here. I want to work with the maitre d'."

I said, "Sam, I want you to work back here."

In a frustrated tone of voice, he said, "Dad, I can't speak Mexican!" So he ended up working with the maitre d', a guy named Tony, and he got a $13 tip. So Tony said, "Hey Sam, you gotta split that with me." And Sam replied, "Well, if you treated people nice like me, you'd get your own."

It's becoming apparent that Sam, just like his dad, is developing a no-nonsense approach to the business of life. Sam and I were alone together one day just before Christmas, 2004. He said, "Dad, tell me the truth. Is there a Santa Claus?" He caught me a little off guard. "Well, there is . . . in spirit," I said. "There is the spirit of giving at Christmas."

Sam persisted. "Then let me ask you this way. Who gives the presents—the spirit or you?"

"I do," I said.

"Well, then you're the guy I want to talk to," he said.

# 17

# FEEDING A NEED— HUNGER BUSTERS HITS THE STREETS

## **F** *o o d* *f o r* **T** *h o u g h t*

Everybody is someone else's child. I look at every person that way.
They all came into the world deserving love and attention and
guidance. Not all of them got it.

I am blessed a thousand times over. There's not a day that goes by when I don't pause to remind myself of that. Because of my humble upbringing, it's still a little hard to believe that I'm actually wealthy. Lots of times I ask myself, why me? I tell myself, maybe it's because I'm a good person and therefore good things happen to me.

But when I sat down for a long talk in 1999 with my good friend and confidante, Father John Waggoner, the man who baptized my son and administered last rites to my father, I had further cause for reflection. John was about to retire, and we started ruminating about each others' lives. He asked me about the wide variety of people I've served over my career, and he was floored to find out that every day, more than 200,000 people around the world eat meals in restaurants I've created. "That's a lot of influence," he said. "Yeah, it's a big responsibility, too," I replied.

Somehow, my accomplishments rang a little hollow as we continued our talk, as the topic turned to the legions of people out there who weren't so fortunate. Soon, I realized there's one market I hadn't addressed at all in my career, and it's probably the most important one: the homeless, or who I came to call "the forgotten customer." While we have our favorite charities, I haven't done much hands-on work with these organizations, other than to open up my home or my restaurants for occasional fundraisers. Mostly, I just write a check and let other people decide where to put the resources. But, I thought, I'm an active member of this community, and it's been very good to me. I must support it and give something back—and not just money.

Dallas and most other cities, I thought, would rather just sweep the problem of the homeless under the rug than have to address it. But could I really make a difference to them? For a long time, I had thought about opening a soup kitchen, where street people would eat free but where the general public would also eat to help support the place. But I'd never acted on it, I told the priest. We talked about the idea, and I resolved to do a little research. We later concluded that an awful lot of street people can't—or won't—go to soup kitchens and shelters.

So I visited with Clora Hogan, the Dallas area's biggest advocate for the homeless, and she explained why. Many street people look at soup kitchens with distrust, because they are almost exclusively associated with organizations that have an agenda. That is, street people must sit through a religious service, an alcohol-abuse and substance-abuse lecture, or some other kind of homily just to get a meal that is often barely palatable. To some, that's not a worthwhile trade-off, she told me. For this and many other reasons, this segment simply opts to live on the streets full-time and, as a result, eats very poorly.

I'd already been tossing around the name of this venture in my mind, settling on Hunger Busters. But it would take several months to form a workable plan. I concluded that I should approach this with the same philosophy that I employ when I'm conceiving a restaurant: Do a market study and a customer profile and then create points of difference that will serve genuine points of need, and wants, in my patrons. As I dug into this complex issue, one solution finally emerged.

When our new home was being built in Preston Hollow, Lillie and I stood overlooking the construction (my bricklaying days were behind me now). We heard a loud horn honk and watched as a lunch wagon pulled up to the site and the crew hurried over to it for sustenance. "Why not create a soup kitchen on wheels?" Lillie asked. Yes, that's it, I thought. Why not take the food out to the streets instead of making them come to a central location to get it? "Great idea, Lillie," I said.

Clora also liked the idea, and she helped us select areas of town where we'd serve the most homeless people. We concluded that word of our effort would quickly spread on the street, and more and more people would be drawn to these central locations once we began operations. We could buy a large, used delivery truck and convert it to our purposes. But before we could get under way, I had to navigate channels at the city and ran into some bureaucratic resistance at the Dallas Health Department. I learned that giving food away is not as easy as you might think, even for someone with extensive experience in the food-dispensing business.

At first, I talked with a by-the-book guy at the very bottom of the health department's totem pole and told him about our plans. "You can't do it this way," he said. "Not with a used truck." He reeled off a mind-boggling list of requirements, including refrigeration, sinks, hot water, etc. Wow. The price tag of a new truck with all these features would be about $60,000. "But all we are going to do is distribute packaged food and containers of soups," I said. "There will be no cooking on it. We will prepare all of this in our restaurants, which have been inspected and certified by the board of health. It will be safe and sanitary and healthy. We're not selling it. We're going to give this stuff away."

He said, "Well, those are the rules, Mr. Romano. If you don't like it, you're going to have to go above me." So we did. It took a while, but we finally found a higher-up in the food chain—a woman who listened intently to our plan and finally said, "No problem, Phil, do it. We appreciate your effort. Just don't get anybody sick."

So we formed The Food Foundation with the help of Clora and another homeless advocate, Casey Coda, and bought an old FedEx van to convert into our rolling Hunger Busters soup kitchen. Only we wouldn't be ladling up any old concoction. We'd serve hearty soup made freshly at eatZi's and sandwiches made freshly at Nick & Sam's—not from expiring inventory, by the way. We'd also give out fruit and other nutritious goodies, including cookies, given to us courtesy of Aphrodite Sweet Temptations.

So we finally took our Hunger Busters idea to the streets, starting out in late 2000 with runs each Wednesday. Our stops included sites across from the main Dallas Public Library branch and in the parking lot of the old Sportatorium pro wrestling arena. Lillie would drive the truck, and Sam would ride along with us to help. At first, the homeless were skeptical about our presence. What's the catch, they asked? From experience, they suspected we must have some ulterior motive.

But we weren't about to tell them they needed to turn their lives around. We aren't miracle workers. We just wanted to help keep these folks alive until they found a way to turn things around. If asked why I'm doing this, I'd just say it's my humanitarian and patriotic duty. This isn't a government program, and it's not the government's community. It's our community. The government would like to feed the homeless, but in reality it can't. So citizens have to step up. And many have. We watched our own volunteer base grow quickly.

Sam got an eyeful. It was good lesson, not only to see that many people in this world aren't nearly as fortunate as him, but that he could make a difference in their lives with donations of time, effort, and resources. Even now, with every dollar he gets at home, I have him do three things: save a third of it, give a third to charity, and do what he wants with the rest. I want him to respect money and help people with it. To me, that's money in the bank, both monetarily and intrinsically.

Each week, more and more homeless came to greet the Hunger Busters truck. The "soup line" was starting to lengthen. By late 2004, we were serving more than 1,500 a week! It was like building a business. We learned to cater to our customers' needs. When we first started running, we were handing out apples, but they weren't getting eaten. We found out why. These folks either had no teeth or very bad teeth, and they weren't up to the challenge of getting through an apple. So we started passing out bananas instead.

From late fall through early spring in North Texas, it's amazing how cold it can get out there at night. I often find myself shivering just when I'm handing out food. Imagine how these people feel sleeping out here every night, I thought. So we started passing out blankets, socks, and other clothing. The Army-Navy Surplus store on McKinney Avenue in Dallas donated a bunch of fatigues and coats, while other businesses stepped up with donations. The executive director of Hunger Busters, a very committed woman named Tina Williams, goes to corporations to recruit donations and volunteers. Some of these companies also pull together excess soap and other toiletries that their employees who travel a lot have amassed from their trips.

Most of the Hunger Busters recipients have no idea who I am or what I've done, and they probably don't care. A lot of them just call me Mr. Phil. But they do appreciate our food and tell us so. The vitamin-packed soups, such as our sweet potato-and-corn chowder, get rave reviews from our patrons. One local writer called the meals "the down-and-out's version of a gourmet dinner."

The street people we serve often volunteer tales of how they got where they are. Some of them are mentally ill and just stopped taking their medication, while others are substance abusers. Many are simply disenfranchised and choose to live this way. But most of the homeless we meet have simply experienced a run of bad luck that may have included job loss, divorce, debilitating accident, death in the family, or some other major psychological blow. And 46 percent of them are women and children.

A down-on-her-fortune woman named "Shelly" is a good example. She was employed in the accounting department of Sears's national claims center for five years. But both her parents grew gravely ill, so she sold her home to provide live-in care for them. After her mother's death, Shelly became very depressed, and her husband divorced her. Teetering on the brink, she soon suffered a nervous breakdown that led to her job loss. Her father died shortly after that. She became increasingly distraught, and her ex-husband claimed she was an unfit parent, then took away their nine-year-old daughter. Shelly was just crushed and went downhill fast, eventually finding herself living under a bridge. If not for Hunger Busters, she wouldn't eat on many days. She tells us that our visits also make her feel less frightened and isolated and says she's working on getting her life back together.

One homeless man, "Ronald," was earning $50,000 a year installing network systems for AT&T until he started feeling the delayed effects of a fall from a two-story building. Doctors told him that his spine had been severely misaligned in the accident, causing nerve damage to both legs and even some heart damage. Soon, Ronald was partially paralyzed, and he lost his job in October of 2002. He had no work, no prospects, no health benefits, and no disability coverage. His marriage ended, and he soon found himself living on the street in a wheelchair. He became a regular on our Hunger Busters route, and we provided him with both nourishment and emotional support. He eventually recovered enough to start walking with a cane. He asked us one day: "Is eatZi's hiring?" For him, we were. He started work there in January of 2004 and enrolled in culinary studies at El Centro College in Dallas. One day, he plans to start his own catering company. He does a great job for eatZi's, too.

But there are tragic tales, too. There was a very nice Native American man from Arizona who I saw on the Hunger Busters route three times a week. He apparently had a serious drinking problem, but everybody in our organization really seemed to like him. One day, we got the unfortunate news that he had been hit by a car and killed. His tribe and his brother, who had not seen him in a very long time, were contacted, but they didn't have the money to ship him home. But it was very important in their culture to get the body back right away, so they went out and borrowed $2,500 from the bank. I sent them a check to cover their loan. People who are suffering with such a loss shouldn't have to endure additional financial pressure unnecessarily.

The street folks are almost always good-hearted. In our first Hunger Busters run after 9/11, we put out a can to benefit the victims fund. It was quite touching to see how some of the homeless were actually putting in what little change they had. One woman even asked if we could accept an unopened can of beer. "Sure," I said. No matter how much they said they hated the government and other institutions, these folks were still willing to pitch in to help through them. It made me realize that the homeless were also patriotic citizens of our country. We also came to find out that about 40 percent of the men were Vietnam veterans.

My wife will be the first to tell you that I sleep restlessly at night, and I guess that's because my mind is always abuzz. But on nights I go out on runs with my Hunger Busters colleagues, I'm out like a light as soon as I hit the pillow. I've come to understand that the people who get the most pleasure out of charity are those who give directly to the recipient, not the ones who write out the checks. And Hunger Busters is probably the most fulfilling thing I've ever done, because I am so actively involved. We have expanded our program, acquired a newer truck, which a guy by the name of Randy Wellborn of Complete Restaurant Services (CRS) finished out for us from the goodness of his heart. Sign Pros of Dallas did our logos for us. It's a collective effort. We added more stopping points and more nights, with the eventual goal of running routes five nights a week. We keep Hunger Busters a lean organization. Lillie, God bless her, handles a lot of the administration of the Dallas operation, and we employ just one paid staffer, Tina, who has a passion for her job, really cares about the people we serve, and is willing to do whatever is necessary to make the whole thing work. I continue to ride along. The groups of homeless are always waiting for us when we arrive. We feed hundreds every night we go out. Many who we meet along our four stops on the backstreets of Dallas tell us they just wouldn't eat if not for us. Since we started Hunger Busters, the number of homeless grew from 3,000 in late 2000 to more than 6,000 in early 2005.

Hunger Busters landed us on the CBS *Evening News* once and in several other broadcasts as well as spreads in *People* magazine and other national publications. The University of North Texas gave me its first-ever Gateway award for business, community, and humanitarian efforts for Hunger Busters, and the Texas Restaurant Association and Greater Dallas Restaurant, as well as other organizations, have given me similar honors. Though I appreciate the recognition, it's not a motivator in all this.

I felt all along that this was an idea with "legs"—meaning it could expand to other cities and states. In fact, we've started to receive inquiries from all over the country. I'd love to see more cities and states use our Hunger Busters name to promote fundraising to do this or to get their own programs rolling. There's no better time than the present. People who want to see what we can do can visit http://www.hungerbustersdallas.org.

One particular Hunger Busters run sticks out in my mind. It had been a busy night, we were at our last stop, and I was a little tired. Out of the corner of my eye, I noticed a neatly dressed man getting out of a car nearby. I watched as he quickly made his way over to the van. I muttered, "What the hell, is that guy trying to get a free meal off of us?" But he didn't seem interested in the food. Instead, he came directly to me. "You probably don't remember me," he said. "But a couple of months ago, I was down on my luck, and I was one of those people standing in that line over there. I just wanted to come by and tell you that things are better now. I've got a good job and a good car, and it dawned on me that I never properly thanked you for what you did for me. So thank you. Thank you."

That night, I slept like a rock.

# 18

# IL MULINO—NEW YORK'S FINEST HEADS WEST

**F** o o d   f o r   **T** h o u g h t

The food critics I most respect are my customers. I measure their
regard in the dollars they spend, their compliments to the staff, and
the word of mouth they spread to their friends.

**I**'ve bankrolled other people's
ideas over the years, but when it comes to opening restaurants,
I usually prefer to use my own ideas. This way, I can assure creative and operational continuity, food consistency, and unwa-
vering dedication to the points of difference needed to make it
unique. But in 2002, I got an offer that I couldn't refuse—from
an Italian family in New York City, no less.

Il Mulino, a Greenwich Village landmark that Zagat has
ranked as the top restaurant in New York City for 20 of 23 years
since its debut in 1981, has obviously done some amazing numbers, despite its cramped location and a seating capacity of less
than 100. Because the tables are so close together, people almost have to crawl over one another to come and go. But they
don't mind. The fine dining restaurant is always full, its Old
World cuisine fashioned from the Abruzzo region of Italy to

absolute perfection, and weekend reservations can take months to secure, despite a price range that's top of the scale.

Brothers Fernando and Gino Masci, the culinary geniuses behind the place, have been approached dozens of times over the years about replicating Il Mulino (The Water Mill) in other cities. But they weren't entirely comfortable that another restaurateur would treat their singular concept and distinct brand right, or possess the know-how to replicate Il Mulino. But the Mascis joined forces with investors Jerry Katzoff and Brian Gallagher, who they felt had the foresight and the ability to grow Il Mulino's. Those two contacted me in late 2002 to talk about that very subject.

Of course, it was crucial to find a good location, so I told the two that I'd give them a jingle if I found the right one. It wasn't long before I did. As luck would have it, a perfect building had recently become available in uptown Dallas, at 2408 Cedar Springs Road. It was a spacious spot that housed the former Casa Dominguez restaurant, and it was only about a block away from Nick & Sam's. I calculated that it would seat 130, or about twice the number the Mascis could accommodate in New York. That capacity was a must in Dallas for this type of concept. New Yorkers will wait an hour and a half or even two hours for a table, but Texans won't, especially if they're paying top dollar for a fine dining experience. Hell, they might even sue me!

Later, when I met Fernando and Gino, I was impressed. With their Italian heritage and mine, the chemistry was perfect. They told me that, aside from resident New York–area patrons, visitors from Texas had by far been Il Mulino's best customers over the years. For about a year, we talked about the possibilities of a Dallas location. I invited them to Dallas, where they visited Nick & Sam's and eatZi's and met my Nick & Sam's partner, Joseph Palladino, who was interested in partnering with me in this venture as well.

I wasn't doing this for the money. I knew this would not only be a great restaurant for Dallas—one that would enhance the city's international fine dining reputation—but as a diner, I also knew I could take my family, friends, and business associates there as often as I wanted, and we would be assured of a fantastic dining experience each time. The Mascis told me they liked what we were doing and felt completely confident that we would treat their brand and reputation properly. So we shook on it.

So there we were, a couple of Italian guys, making a restaurant deal with another couple of Italian guys. The Mascis told us it was like keeping Il Mulino in the family. Well, it didn't take long to attract ten investors for the Dallas location—and those ten stand to do pretty well with this deal, I think. Still, there are no slam dunks in this business: You're only as good as your last meal, as I've always said. But Dallas would be getting some great meals when Il Mulino opened, because we were going to do this thing right.

The location was also ideal because it was directly across the street from our semiprivate nightclub, Medici's, which Joseph and I felt we had to open to keep our Nick & Sam's customers happy. I say "had to open," because in the spring of 2003, Dallas Mayor Laura Miller rammed through a smoking ban covering all the city's restaurants. Any establishment that made more than 25 percent of its revenues from food had to ban smoking entirely, even in their bar and lounge areas, unless they were willing to completely seal them off from the dining area. In most good restaurants, that kind of separation is virtually impossible to pull off, and that goes for Nick & Sam's, where many of our good customers liked to retreat to the bar for a smoke or two after a good meal. An enclosed bar area, aside from becoming practically invisible to customers seated in the main dining room, really disrupts the flow of a well-designed restaurant and robs it of some of its energy.

Before Joseph and I finalized our Il Mulino deal, we decided to spend about $1 million to open the sexy, sleek, and very upscale nightspot, Medici, which is Italian for *royal family*. Medici would complement Nick & Sam's and, eventually, Il Mulino, and patronage at either restaurant would entitle the dining party entrance to the place and royal treatment. It was a new twist on the old crossmarketing strategy I'd used with the Key Hole back in Florida. We finished out Medici in 1940s retro, with brushed, dark-wood walls; burgundy velvet drapes; and overstuffed leather chairs and couches, as well as a posh VIP section. We'd specialize in premium wine and high-end liquor and offered a limited appetizer menu. (We had to be sure our food revenue didn't top Mayor Laura's 25 percent mark.) And, of course, you could fire up at will at Medici—cigars, cigarettes, pipes—you name it. I'm not a big fan of smoking, as I've noted, but I do believe in a person's right to indulge in an appropriate setting.

Medici opened in October of 2003. We decided to use an elevator entry system to create a psychological impression that diners were "going up" when they entered. The elevator separates them, both physically and symbolically, from the humdrum. The walls are decorated with striking, black-and-white Helmut Newton photos, including some of his classic nudes, and we put slightly more provocative photos in the men's room, which would come to be conversation pieces. But it's a high-class place, and it's patronized by a lot of movers and shakers in the 30-and-over set, both male and female. To take advantage of peak after-dinner business and put our best foot forward, the place is only open from 9:00 PM to 2:00 AM, Wednesday through Saturday—but it does a brisk traffic in those hours. We also have some great private parties.

Soon, though, we'd turn our full attention to the main attraction across the street—the nation's second Il Mulino. When we cut the deal, the Masci brothers agreed to split their time between the New York and Dallas locations to get the new location open. They were excited at the prospect of having enough room to demonstrate their skills with a little tableside cooking showmanship—something they couldn't do in the limited confines of their New York venue.

Our challenge was a daunting one: to bring the best restaurant in New York to Dallas. But it was the kind of pressure I absolutely thrive on. To create an extraordinary product, I knew our preparation would also have to be extraordinary. So we hired a young man, Michael Abruzese, who had graduated from a culinary school in New York, and sent him to meet the brothers. Oddly enough, they soon realized that their families both came from the same village in Italy. Their chemistry was tremendous, and the Mascis took Michael under their wings. He trained six months under them there. We also sent 20 other people—chefs, waiters, and managers—up to New York to train with the Mascis, renting several apartments there at a lofty sum. This was no time to be cutting corners. The food would have to be the same as what's served at the New York restaurant to be credible. Only the surroundings would be different. And we would have to give people as good an experience or even better than in the original. Il Mulino would be dramatic—a savored night out in the classic sense.

The Dallas restaurant would be opulent with Old World elegance. We'd have original, still-life oil paintings; imported furnishings and chandeliers; high ceilings; ornate draperies; terracotta dining room walls; large, Roman-themed wall plates; white-clothed tables; and even marble restrooms. Costs exceeded $1.5 million. We'd be open for dinner only, six nights a week, jacket required. Waiters would wear white ties and carry little torches from table to table to help them guide our patrons through the vast menu, which would be a virtual twin to the one at New York's Il Mulino. Entrées would range from $30 to $50, but portions would be huge. And we'd offer complimentary garlic bread, Italian sausage, bruchetta, and thinly sliced fried zucchini to diners as soon as they sat down, plus free, fresh Parmigiano-Reggiano cheese. We'd uncork some of the best and most diverse wines in the world. Fruit-flavored grappa would be offered at the end of the meal, gratis.

The buzz surrounding this place, and the anticipation of it, were unprecedented for me. We had 6,000—yes, 6,000—reservations before we even opened the doors. Locals who had dined at the New York Il Mulino were just ecstatic to be getting this kind of place in their town, assuming they could get in!

We opened Il Mulino New York in February of 2004 to long-reserved full houses. Our chefs had undergone more rigorous training for Il Mulino than any fine dining establishment I had ever been involved with, and I have been pretty demanding. Fernando and Gino, who had spent months in Dallas to shepherd this creation, made sure everything was perfect. Customers told us they found the food to be every bit as good as in New York and welcomed the additional elbow room. Diners raved about such dishes as homemade ravioli with black truffles in champagne sauce, veal scallopini, shellfish, giant lobster, osso buco, chilled baby octopus salad and Zabaglione, and a special marsala-flavored custard prepared in copper cookware tableside.

There were few, if any, complaints about the price, although we did take a little good-natured ribbing about it. Not long after we opened, a good friend of mine was in the middle of dinner and started breaking out into a cold sweat. He was having trouble breathing and passed out. We feared he was having a heart attack. By the time medics arrived, he was alert and feeling better and told me, "Sorry, Phil, I don't usually faint until after I get the bill!"

Il Mulino continues to knock 'em dead in Dallas. People come from hundreds of miles away to get to us. The reservation list is still a very long one, and that tells us everything we need to know about how our customers feel about us.

# 19

# CONCEIVING AT 65

## F o o d   f o r   T h o u g h t

"Being creative is a gift from God, and using that creativity is
a gift back to God." That's what I told an industry gathering when
I was honored with the Innovator of the Year award from
*Nation's Restaurant News* ten years ago for Cozymel's. I wished then,
and now, that all the creative people in the world would resolve
to use their gift throughout their lifetimes.

I'll turn 66 this fall, an age when many people are dreaming about idle hours and packing up their offices. But I'm still at work, because my office is in my head. And as far as I'm concerned, the lights are on and there's extra life in the bulb.

As I was approaching my 60th birthday in the summer of 1999, I was sitting with my lawyer and my accountant, talking about the things I wanted to do in the coming years. "Wait a minute, Phil. I thought you were going to slow down?" said one. "Yeah, I thought you were gonna take it easy," the other chimed in.

And I told them, "Well, you know, I just can't do that, guys. Here I am now with a son who's going to be in my plans from now on. Sure, I'm going to start enjoying myself a little bit more, but now I'm enjoying Sam more than I could enjoy traveling or anything else. I want to stay here while he's in school. So I have to do something—not just hang around."

Well here it is, almost six years later in 2005, and I'm not slowing down one iota. I've been given a gift. It's a sin not to use it, and that's the way I'll look at things the rest of my life, I hope. Today, the devotion I have for a new concept reminds me of the passion I had in my younger days during a new love relationship. I'd meet an attractive woman and fall for her, and there was excitement and passion, and I couldn't get her off my mind. I get the same feeling today for a new restaurant concept. It's a love affair. I devote all my effort and waking hours to it; it constantly occupies my thoughts. I nurture it along, and I have a great passion for it. And as when I was young, when my passion leaves for that relationship for whatever reason, I'll just go off and start another one.

As much as I've changed, I'm still a boy at heart. But I do have a new nickname, courtesy a few of my childhood friends. I've stayed especially close to three buddies with whom I went to grade school, and we were getting together at the wedding of one of their daughters in upstate New York. Before flying out there, my wife and I decided it would be fun to invite all of these guys—David DelloStritto, Joe Daloi, and Vince Ianone— and their wives to celebrate one of my recent birthdays in a very special venue. So I bought plane tickets for everybody but didn't say anything until I got them all together at the same table during the wedding reception, where I said, "Gentlemen. I got a proposition for you. I'd like all of you to come to my birthday celebration. I've got the plane tickets already. I'll pay for everything and for everyone, wives included. Oh, and it's in Florence, Italy!" They looked delighted and flabbergasted. But I added, "There's just one condition: everybody has to go or no deal." They apparently set about coordinating their schedules pretty quickly, because not long after that, they were all winging to Italy.

Well, Lillie and I got there ahead of time and met them in Florence. The first day we checked into the hotel, the clerk started talking Italian to us, and we all looked at her funny. It was obvious we didn't speak the language. "My God, you have Italian names, here you are in Italy, and you can't speak Italian. You ought be ashamed of yourselves," she said. We explained to her that our parents never taught us Italian because they wanted us to be American-Italians, not Italian-Americans. There we were again, revisiting our youth.

As for that nickname, when one of these guys' kids gets married, I have a tradition of giving an untraditional present—a shoebox full of 5,000 one dollar bills. It's always an amusing scene when the bride or groom who's marrying into one of their families opens the gift at the wedding. Here they are, joining an Italian family, and all of a sudden they get a shoebox full of cash. The cash, the friends say, is from that "Romano Soprano."

My own company, Romano Concepts, which I created in 2000, has plenty of things going for it, including Il Mulino, Nick & Sam's, and, of course, Hunger Busters, which we hope to expand nationally to feed the scores of homeless in other cities. EatZi's is also expanding, and that will require a lot of my attention. I also inked a partnership recently with Compass Group North America, the world's largest contract food service provider. They want me to help them develop new business in the Southwest, and I guess I have a few connections they may find useful. They're part of a huge, British-based parent, Compass Group PLC, which generates $17 billion in revenue annually servicing sports arenas and stadiums, airports, universities, museums, performing-arts halls, hospitals, and other venues and also operates high-end restaurants in California, New York, and Chicago.

And, oh yes, there's this little hamburger place I recently invented called Who's Who Burger. A friend of mine told me that he didn't want to renew the lease of his tenant in a small space at Preston Road and Mockingbird Lane in Highland

Park Village, and he asked me if I had any ideas, so I put my mind to creating something unique there. Because there weren't a whole lot of good hamburger places in Highland Park, I did some research and came up with a product that is as delicious as you'll ever taste.

Who's Who uses beef from Wagyu cattle called Kobe beef, a strain that originated in Kobe, Japan. Kobe beef is an incredibly well marbled, flavorful delicacy that requires special cooking. You'll pay a premium for a Kobe Burger, but its flavor is fantastic and its fat content is healthier than any other ground beef. Who's Who also serves hot dogs, turkey cranberry burgers, and veggie portobello burgers. The unique Kobe product is Who's Who's main point of difference, although for a $100 donation to Hunger Busters, patrons can place their autograph on the walls right next to lots of celebrity signatures.

I'm pondering a new Italian concept, too. I want to do an Italian version of Pei-Wei and take my Sicilian friend, Matteo Bartolotta, with me to Italy to research traditional dishes and collect some Old World recipes. Macaroni Grill was Americanized Italian. This will be Italian Italian. We will import everything from Italy. I'm thinking about calling it Pasta-Toots. That should raise a few eyebrows. We'll have extremely big meatballs and T-shirts that say, "I got the biggest balls in town at Pasta-Toots." There'll be Pasta-Toots on every corner. When we close every night, we'll put a sign on the door that says, "Closed. Beat it!" Had you going, didn't I?

I am truly devising the Italian concept, however.

And those are just my food ventures. Dr. Julio Palmaz, my famous stent partner, and I just sold a partnership to Johnson & Johnson. Plus, I'm involved in something new in the field of obesity clinics. A couple of doctors who are weight-control specialists came to me recently with a compelling proposal. They weren't very happy with the radical surgical process called stomach stapling, which is irreversible and has a 2 percent mortality rate. Patients are in the hospital at least four days after such a procedure, and the cost is $30,000, plus they'll never really eat a full meal again. The doctors filled me in on a better approach to severe obesity known as gastric banding, a process where a band is snugly wrapped around the bottom of the esophagus. This can be done laparoscopically on an outpatient basis. This banding creates a small pouch that limits the amount of food intake. The narrowed opening between that pouch and the rest of the stomach also controls how quickly food passes to the lower part of the stomach.

The patient eats less and the time it takes for food to digest is increased—and ravenous hunger is controlled. Later, the opening between the pouch and the lower stomach can be adjusted according to the patient's condition by deflating or inflating the band via the addition or removal of fluid through an easily accessible "port," placed under the skin during the initial procedure. The doctors felt they could open up clinics in the Dallas-Fort Worth areas, and throughout Texas, with a little capital. So I invested in their idea, and we bought out a Dallas surgical center and renamed it the American Institute of Gastric Banding. By the end of 2005, we expect to have additional clinics operating in Fort Worth, Houston, San Antonio, and Austin by the same American Institute name. We've found a niche, we're doing something good for people's health, plus we're giving them a psychological lift that will help them become happier and more productive citizens. As I've said, success comes not only from understanding what will and won't work but how broad a market it will affect. And obesity is a huge, growing problem, no pun intended. The gastric-banding clinics can't help but be a success. By the time this book is published, I may have sold this company, too.

I'm also on several boards, including that of the Cox School of Business at Southern Methodist University, the M.D. Anderson Cancer Center, and the Dallas Homeless Coalition. I lecture at universities, national business conferences, civic organizations, and special interest organizations. How's that for a leisurely retirement?

Plus, I'm having tremendous fun helping raise Sam. He's a never-ending source of joy for his proud Italian pop. Year by year, he becomes more aware of his Italian roots. I've told him that in Italian law, you don't tattletale. One day, I was taking him and some of his friends to a party, and one of the kids started ratting on another for some trivial thing. I said, "Are you tattle-taling back there?" And Sam chimes in, "Dad, dad. It's okay. He's not Italian."

Sometimes, I feel like I'm the luckiest first-generation American-Italian kid on the block myself, living the American dream. For my efforts, industry gurus have called me "the Steven Spielberg of the restaurant industry," "a man possessed to discover 1,001 ways people can enjoy a meal" and "King of Show." I'm the only person in the restaurant industry to create six national concepts. I've opened 28 different restaurant concepts in my 40-plus years in the food industry. My restaurant creations alone have generated more than $10 billion in sales thus far.

Other ideas are still simmering on the burner. My greatest concept may be out there lurking. I have a love affair with the general public, and I want to make them happy. I don't believe I'll ever be too old to formulate, reinvent, nurture, or experiment with a restaurant, still learn a thing or two—and enjoy myself in the process. It's little wonder that my favorite showbiz saying is, "Keep 'em hungry for more."

# A

# MORE FOOD
# FOR THOUGHT—
# PHIL YOUR PLATE

**M**y customers, restaurant industry colleagues, and other businesspeople often pepper me with questions about my creative process, my hiring practices, my likes and dislikes, and how and why I do some of the crazy things I do. So here are a few answers to some frequently asked questions.

*Q: Who do you admire in the industry?*

*A:* Norman Brinker, for one. But there's also a guy named Rich Melman, owner of the Chicago-based Lettuce Entertain You, who's one of my favorite restaurant innovators. We partnered on a number of projects. We have a lot in common. Neither of our families had any money when we were growing up, and we both basically came out of nowhere. Then there's Rick Federico, CEO of P.F. Chang's, who helped grow Macaroni Grill while he was with Brinker, and Russell Owens, president of Pei Wei. I also admire Creed Ford and Lane Cardwell. And I have a lot of respect for the chefs and managers who make everything work.

*Q: What trends do you see developing in the U.S. restaurant industry?*

*A:* A lot of independently owned Asian and Italian restaurants have been dying out. It's not so much because of competition from the chains; it's more because the families running them have kids who go off to college to become professionals in other walks of life, and they don't return, leaving mom and pop little choice but to fold up their tent. It's hard to find people who want to buy out an old restaurant operation that's been under family ownership.

But people still have a yearning for distinctive cooking. As ma and pa close shop, the demand for their distinctive, family-recipe-style food remains. So there are entrepreneurial opportunities out there. Some managers working at Macaroni Grill and Olive Garden are stopping and thinking, "If I can do it for someone else, I can do it for myself." That philosophy has a familiar ring to it, if you look at my background. Some of these guys are departing to open their own Italian restaurants. Many of them are quite good. The industry needs that continuous stream of creativity and nonconformity.

*Q: How do you get into a creative frame of mind?*

*A:* By daydreaming, usually. As a kid, I used to lie on the floor during those pretelevision days and listen to the radio, and it really stimulated my imagination. Kids and a lot of young adults now aren't forced to use their imagination in the same capacity. They let television, video games, and computers do the thinking and creating and dreaming for them. Sometimes, I can just lie in bed daydreaming and still be at work. I call it "living in my mind." I'm devising my next concept, strategizing, tweaking, projecting, saying "what if?" and "why not?"—even with my eyes closed. Especially with my eyes closed.

Also, I love to discuss my creative ideas with my customers—not just a bunch of jaded restaurant operations people. I imagine how exciting my next concept will be when it finally becomes a reality. And if I can get customers to think in the same vein with me and they get excited, I know I'm on to something.

### Q: Do you have any hobbies?

A: Restaurants are my real hobby, besides being a dad. But I also love to paint and have a little studio in uptown Dallas, where my son often joins me for a rousing creative session. My art has come to mirror my life. One writer for *Texas Monthly* called me a "frustrated abstract expressionist." The only time I can really focus on painting is when I don't have a major project going and can do a bunch of paintings at once. Then I stop and absorb some more of the world, which will be reflected the next time I return to the canvas.

People say that my homes in Dallas and in New York have come to be "Fisher Price-like" because of their vibrant colors and cheerful décor—some of which includes my own paintings. I also try to support new artists and keep an eye out for talent. Personally, I'm inspired by artists such as Jackson Pollock, Salvador Dali, Peter Max, Mark Rothko, Vincent van Gogh, and Robert Motherwell.

I also look for people who want to carve a niche in this business. In a new concept, I remind candidates they will be starting off on the ground floor. I like the attitude that "if this works, then there's nothing but blue sky ahead of us." I want decision makers, not lackeys. The leadership end has to come from the top. When I start a concept, I know that nobody will care about my business more than me, because I gave birth to it. Nobody will work harder than me to make sure it succeeds. So how can anyone expect their employees to care about their business more than them? I tell employees that they should work hard because they are working for themselves and not just "for Phil." I tell them that no one works for me. Everyone works with me. If they work hard, they will succeed with me or with someone else.

*Q: What about firing people. Is it hard for you?*

*A:* I never fire employees. They fire themselves. When they come on board, they understand what they're supposed to do and what the end result of their actions should be. I have a responsibility to show them that explicitly and offer them a little creative latitude in how they want to get the job done.

They now have accountability but not to me or the restaurant—to themselves. The main thrust of this approach is to get workers to take ownership of what they do. I get my employee and management groups together and find ways to give them a percentage of the business. They're owners. They're making it happen for themselves as well as me.

*Q: When you're building a restaurant, how close is your final product to your original plans?*

*A:* Sometimes it changes a hell of a lot. If something seems to be headed in the wrong direction, I'll change it without hesitation. In fact, I've become famous for tearing things up at the last minute, often to the chagrin of construction workers, accountants, and operations people. Blueprints be damned. I've had ovens torn out, artwork totally redone, walls knocked down, and cash stands moved because I didn't think they conformed with my original vision. It's far better to suffer a little inconvenience and expense in the near term than it is to settle for an inferior product that you know you'll be stuck with and probably have to change later anyway.

**Q: *How do you go about becoming an entrepreneur?***

*A:* Go to work in the particular industry you're interested in. If it's insurance, for example, you must first know it, understand it, live it, and work it to experience the problems and challenges of the field. Come up with a solution to resolve those issues. Then go off and become an entrepreneur, develop those solutions, and sell them to that industry. That will be your point of difference. If you are committed to the restaurant business and want to do a steakhouse, then focus exclusively on steakhouses. Go to other steak places. Ask people who dine out frequently what they like and don't like, what displeases them or what needs and wants they have that are not being fulfilled by other restaurants. Keep a record of your findings. Jot down your own ideas as you go and collect them as well. Some ideas will be crazy, but some may turn out to be ingenious. The most successful entrepreneurs march to a different beat. They're men or women who strongly dislike the thought of having to get up every morning with the fear that someone could fire them.

Famous investor Warren Buffett once noted: "Somebody is sitting in the shade today only because somebody planted a tree a long time ago." So remember this: 100 percent of the businesses in the United States had to be started by somebody. And all of the businesses of the future will also have to be started by somebody. When you consider that 99 percent of these businesses are small businesses, there will always be room for good ideas created by entrepreneurs. You can always find professional managers to run them, but somebody has to start them.

**Q: *Have you experienced any challenges from having a child so late in life?***

*A:* No, I'm in great health, I work out vigorously every day and have no trouble helping my wife, Lillie, keep up with Sam.

I do take a little flack for having a kid that young, though. Sometimes I wear a shirt that says, "No, I'm NOT the grandfather."

*Q: What would you have done if you didn't get into the restaurant industry?*

*A:* People say I should have been a stand-up comedian. I do have a wry sense of humor, in part from being in this business so long. I've hosted some pretty wild parties in my restaurants over the years. Once, an 85-year-old guy was having a birthday party, and we hired a woman to jump out of a giant cake naked. Out she came and said to him, "Would you like some super sex, baby?" The old man replied, "I'll take the soup." No, that really didn't happen.

*Q: What's your favorite food?*

*A:* My request for a last meal: a hot dog with mustard.

# B

# PHIL ROMANO'S FOOD CONCEPTS

## CHRONOLOGY

*1965, The Gladiator in Lake Park, Florida.* First Romano restaurant, Italian-American, opened at age 24 with a partner after selling off 2 karate schools. Later bought out partner on a loan from his father, who mortgaged his house to foot the bill. Started with $7,000.

*1968, Nag's Head Pub in West Palm Beach, Florida.* English-style bar and restaurant, opened with two partners. Featured first Romano demonstration kitchen and one of the first salad bars in the country. Also featured giant, personalized beer mugs that were presold to raise more start-up capital. Started out with three investors pitching in $2,000 each. Bought out by partners for $50,000.

*1969, The Key Hole in Palm Beach, Florida.* Upscale, members-only bar with key-access only. A TV camera at the front door with a monitor inside alerted patrons to who was entering.

Engraved customer names on bar for a charitable donation. Wall-to-wall portraits of customers. Closed the place to open Romano's 300 across the street. Started with $2,000.

*1970, Romano's 300 in Palm Beach, Florida.* Medieval English-themed fine dining restaurant. Members-only by day, open to the public at night. Winner of the exclusive *Holiday Magazine* Dining Excellence award three consecutive years. Regular haunt of Jordan's King Hussein when he was in town. Started with SBA loan. Memberships sold for additional working capital.

*1974, Friends of Edinburgh Eating & Drinking Society in Vero Beach, Florida.* Pub-style eatery with elaborate international menus that were shipped to Scotland, postmarked, and then returned for authenticity. Funded by partners and investors.

*1974, Shuckers—A Real Good Seafood Place in West Palm Beach, Florida.* Originally to be named Mother Shuckers. First seafood restaurant in area to serve giant lobster. Pioneered side servings of red-jacket potatoes and corn on the cob. Bought seafood by the truckload directly from fishermen. Sold company in Swiss francs. Funded by investors.

*1974, First National Bar & Grill in West Palm Beach, Florida.* Restaurant and nightclub on bottom floor of office tower. Charged by the minute for lunch. Opened talent company, First National Productions, with high school friend, actor Burt Reynolds.

*1975, Pasta Palace in Lake Worth, Florida.* Movie house turned restaurant. Terraced seating, silent movies, menu on screen. Visible pasta machine. Deli in front lobby. Funded by investors.

*1977, Shuckers—A Real Good Seafood Place in San Antonio, Texas.* First Texas venture. Same concept as Florida Shuckers. Was minority partner. Funded by investors.

*1978, Enoch's in San Antonio, Texas.* Private dining club specializing in steak and fish. Limited menu. Served only 100 to 125 dinners a night. Started with $35,000.

*1979, Barclay's in San Antonio, Texas.* Private bar and backgammon club. Piano bar, backgammon tournaments, in-house library. Sold 1,500 memberships at $100 apiece to start.

*1980, Fuddruckers in San Antonio, Texas.* First national concept. Upscale hamburger restaurant featuring exhibition cooking, on-premises bakery, and butcher shop. Created Hamburger Appreciation Society of North America (HASNA). Original investors putting up $15,000 earned $3.4 million each 18 months after the chain was founded. Sold majority interest in 1986.

*1986, Stix Eating Spa in San Antonio, Texas.* Healthy-eating establishment featuring kebabs, Yakitori cooking, and long, exhibition charbroil cookers. Nonsmoking, wine and beer only. Considered ahead of its time. San Antonio demographic could not support it. Started with $1 million.

*1988, Romano's Macaroni Grill in Leon Springs (San Antonio), Texas.* Northern Italian fare, exhibition kitchen, chef-driven operation. Winter and summer menus. Wine by the honor system. Contrast of upscale and downscale design elements. Waiters wrote names upside-down in crayon on white tablecloths. Entrées and salads on display on counters. First Romano concept sold to Brinker International for $5 million in stock in 1989. Currently about 200 in operation. Started with $150,000.

*1989, Texas Tortilla Bakery in New York City, New York.* Partnership with Arthur "Christy" Powers. Bought out Peso's Mexican Food Restaurants in New York with intent to open a chain of taco stands. Texas-style tortillas made from scratch. Plan to give away penny stocks to customers thwarted. Underwriter went out of business. Public company.

*1992, Rudy's Country Store and Bar-B-Que in Leon Springs (San Antonio), Texas.* Barbecue restaurant opened in old filling station/general store building. Wide meat selection, including prime rib that was flavored by oak instead of mesquite. Proprietor "Doc" Holiday's sauce became internationally famous. Concept sold to Creed Ford.

*1992, Nachomama's in Leon Springs (San Antonio), Texas.* Authentic Mexican-Mexican food, the forerunner to Cozymel's. Authentic Mexican dishes, multiple frozen drink machines, zany décor, bilingual wait staff. Started with $10,000. Sold to Brinker, which changed name to Cozymel's, for $7 million.

*1992, Spageddies Italian Italian Food in Dallas, Texas.* Family-oriented Italian restaurant. First Dallas-launched concept. Bocci ball courts. First-time guests were tagged for special treatment. Started as joint venture with Brinker International. Sold share for $6 million to Brinker, which later sold it.

*1995, Rosalie's Cucina & Wine Cellar in Skaneateles, New York.* Venture with sister, Rosalie. Country-Italian cuisine, wood-burning fireplace, wine cellar, outdoor Bocci ball court, herb garden, and Mediterranean-style courtyard. Started with $1.3 million. Sold to current owner after Rosalie passed away from cancer.

*1996, EatZi's in Dallas, Texas.* National restaurant-meal replacement concept featuring fresh restaurant-quality take-out food. Twenty to 40 chefs per unit in kitchen stores. Fifteen hundred different products offered daily. Fifteen to sixteen million dollars in annual sales at Dallas location, including $1 million in wine sales. Approximately 2,500 customers per day in larger units. Started as joint venture with Brinker. Took over as CEO in mid-1999 to direct the company. Partnered with Castanea Partners in 2002 to buy from Brinker.

*1997, Johnny Angel's Heavenly Burgers in Skaneateles, New York.* Burger place similar to Fuddruckers done in partnership with a former classmate who had been unseated from a city post. Appeared in the *Wall Street Journal* and the *New York Times,* on network TV.

*1999, Nick & Sam's in Dallas, Texas.* Fine dining establishment named after son Sam. Free caviar. Did $4 million first full year. Baby grand piano in open kitchen. Arched ceiling. Established as one of the city's best restaurants within months. More than 300 different wines with extensive, readily accessible wine data base for customers that chronicles a vintage's history and compatibility with Nick & Sam's entrées. Started for $1.8 million (property) and $1.5 million for interior.

*1999, Wild About Harry's in Dallas, Texas.* Custard and hot dog shop founded in Highland Park by Dallas resident Harry Coley, using mother's recipe. Old-fashioned-style hot dogs made of beef brisket. Manned, glassed-in custard machine. Opened two new locations late 1999 in Dallas area. Invested $1.4 million. Partnership dissolved.

*2000, Hunger Busters in Dallas, Texas.* Rolling soup kitchen operated by The Food Foundation, founded to feed and clothe Dallas homeless. Plans national rollout.

*2000, Wé/Oui, Oui/Wé—a French Eating Place in Dallas, Texas.* French restaurant in the Crescent Hotel. Belied the French restaurant standard by offering large portions at inexpensive prices. Started with $2.5 million. Now closed.

*2002, Lobster Ranch in Dallas, Texas.* Seafood concept. Started with $600,000 in a partnership. Now closed.

*2002, Who's Who Burger in Dallas, Texas.* Unique hamburger restaurant in Highland Park area of Dallas uses beef from Wagyu cattle, called Kobe beef, a strain originating in Kobe, Japan.

*2004, Il Mulino in Dallas, Texas.* Top-ranked fine dining restaurant in New York opens first location outside of Big Apple. Old World cuisine fashioned from the Abruzzo region of

Italy. Partnered with brothers Fernando and Gino Masci, other investors.

## PHIL ROMANO NATIONAL RESTAURANT CONCEPTS

Fuddruckers

Romano's Macaroni Grill

Rudy's Country Store and Bar-B-Que

Cozymel's Coastal Mexican Grill

Spageddies

eatZi's

## OTHER PHIL ROMANO BUSINESS VENTURES

*Baroni's Italian clothiers.* Opened men's clothing store in San Antonio, Texas, 1980.

*DocuCon.* Formed image processing company in San Antonio, Texas, 1988.

*Leon Springs Dancehall.* Remains open in Leon Springs near San Antonio.

*Venture capitalist.* Bankrolled PALMAZ Stent that was sold to Johnson & Johnson; several versions are still in use for angioplasty surgery and other medical procedures.

*Expandable Graph Partnership.* 1985. (Medical products company in partnership with stent inventor Julio Palmaz)

*ABPS Company.* 2000. (Medical partnership with Julio Palmaz)

*American Institute of Gastric Banding.* Partner in obesity clinics, 2004.

# Share the message!

### Bulk discounts
Discounts start at only 10 copies and range from 30% to 55% off retail price based on quantity.

### Custom publishing
Private label a cover with your organization's name and logo. Or, tailor information to your needs with a custom pamphlet that highlights specific chapters.

### Ancillaries
Workshop outlines, videos, and other products are available on select titles.

### Dynamic speakers
Engaging authors are available to share their expertise and insight at your event.

**Call Dearborn Trade Special Sales at 1-800-621-9621, ext. 4444, or e-mail trade@dearborn.com.**

Dearborn™
Trade Publishing
A **Kaplan Professional** Company